Legends and Stories

FROM THE PACIFIC CREST TRAIL

STEVE STOCKTON

JASON KENT

FREE REIGN

Contents

Introduction

In the stillness of ancient forests, along the ragged edges of towering mountain ranges, and across the vast, echoing expanse of arid deserts, stories are born. The Pacific Crest Trail, a sprawling tapestry of diverse landscapes that stretches 2,650 miles from the sultry confines of the U.S.-Mexico border to the cool, misty embrace of the U.S.-Canada boundary, is not just a trail—it's a storyteller.

Legends and Stories: From the Pacific Crest Trail seeks to unveil the whispered tales that have long remained the secrets of the winds, rivers, and ancient trees. These are not just stories of human endurance and nature's grandeur, but also of the mysteries and legends that have evolved in the trail's embrace. From the time-worn myths of Native American tribes to the modern-day anecdotes of lone hikers, this book captures the essence of a path that has witnessed countless footsteps, each with its own unique story to tell.

As you delve into these pages, you will journey beyond mere geography. You will traverse the realms of time, culture, and the supernatural. This is not merely a collection of tales but an invitation to step into the heart of the Pacific Crest Trail—a place where legends are as real as the rugged trail beneath your feet and where every twist and turn has a story waiting to be told. Welcome to the chronicles of the wild, the mysterious, and the profound. Welcome to the legends and stories from the Pacific Crest Trail.

- Steve Stockton

Manning Park (2655)

• Stehekin (2569)
N. Cascades NP
Glacier Peak
• Stevens Pass (2472)
Seattle •
• Snoqualmie Pass (2396)

Mt. Rainier NP
• White Pass (2298)
Mt. St. Helens •   • Mt. Adams

Portland •
Mt. Hood   • Cascade Locks (2150)

Mt. Jefferson
• Sisters (2002)

• Shelter Cove (1907)

Crater Lake NP

Ashland •
(1721)
• Etna (1600)
Mt. Shasta
Dunsmuir •   • Burney Falls SP (1417)
(1500)
• Old Station (1372)
Lassen NP
• Belden (1283)

• Sierra City (1191)
Lake Tahoe (1089)

• Tuolumne Meadows (937)
Yosemite NP
• Vermilion Valley Resort (871)

Kings Canyon NP
Sequoia NP   • Mt. Whitney

• Kennedy Meadows (697)

• Mojave (564)

Agua   • Wrightwood (366)
Dulce (455)   • Big Bear City (276)
• Palm Springs (151)
Idyllwild (180) •
• Warner Springs (110)

San Diego •
Campo (0)

One

~~~

THE ENIGMA OF THE DARK WATCHERS

NESTLED along the Santa Lucia Mountains in California's Big Sur region, there exists a mystery as ancient as the native tribes that first populated the area. Silhouetted against the twilight sky, figures known as the "Dark Watchers" have been reported by observers for centuries. These elusive, shadowy figures, often spotted at great distances along the ridges and peaks, have become the stuff of local legend and folklore.

Origins:

The origins of the Dark Watchers remain shrouded in mystery. Local Native American tribes, such as the Chumash, have stories and legends that date back over a millennium, some of which make reference to shadowy figures or entities in the mountains. Yet, it's difficult to ascertain whether these tales directly relate to the contemporary Dark Watcher legends or represent different cultural narratives altogether.

Before European settlers arrived in the region, the area was inhabited by the Chumash people for thousands of years. Their rich tapestry of oral tradition and legends provides some potential early references to the Dark Watchers. The Chumash painted intricate cave and rock art, which some believe could depict the enigmatic figures. While direct evidence connecting the Chumash legends to the Dark Watchers is scant, the stories of "nunashish" or otherworldly beings from their folklore might have some parallels.

The Chumash believed in a variety of spiritual entities, both benevolent and malevolent. The mountains and wilderness areas were considered sacred, liminal spaces where the veil between the physical and spiritual world was thin. Entities dwelling in these regions were believed to hold significant power and knowledge.

The phenomenon of the Dark Watchers wasn't restricted to indigenous tales. Early Spanish settlers and explorers in California also had stories of "Los Vigilantes Oscuros" or "The Old Ones" (sometimes referred to as "Los Antiguos"). These figures were said to appear at the end of the day, standing silently and looking out into the distance. Much like later tales, they would vanish the moment someone tried to approach them or looked away.

It's worth noting that the Spanish settlers had no known direct contact with the Chumash in terms of shared legends. This separation makes the similarity in stories even more intriguing and gives credence to the idea that something genuinely unexplained might have been occurring in the mountains.

Over time, with the influx of more settlers, miners during the gold rush, and eventually modern Californians, the stories of the Dark Watchers evolved and merged. Each generation, each group brought its own interpretation and experiences to the legend, enriching it.

As is often the case with folklore, pinpointing a single "origin" is challenging. Stories evolve, intermingle, and change over time based on cultural, environmental, and societal factors. The Dark Watchers legend, with its ancient roots and continued modern sightings, exemplifies this dynamic nature of folklore.

In essence, while the origins of the Dark Watchers remain elusive, their enduring presence in the tales of various cultures and eras speaks to their deep-rooted significance in the region's collective consciousness.

Descriptions:

Witnesses often describe the Dark Watchers as tall, sometimes over ten feet, humanoid figures that stand motionless, gazing out over the valleys and sea. They appear around dusk or dawn, and they always stand in silhouette, making their specific features difficult to discern. Some accounts attribute them with flowing cloaks or wide-brimmed hats, but these details vary.

- Physical Stature

- **Height**: They are frequently described as tall, imposing figures. The height often ranges from being slightly taller than the average human to descriptions of them being giants, standing over 10 feet tall.
- **Silhouette**: The most consistent aspect of the Dark Watchers is their shadowy appearance. They're nearly always described as dark, featureless silhouettes. This makes discerning specific features difficult, and they usually appear this way regardless of the angle of light, which adds to their enigmatic nature.

-Clothing and Attire

- **Cloaks**: One of the most frequently noted details is that these figures often appear to be wearing long, flowing cloaks or robes that billow gently, even when there's no wind.

- **Hats**: In several accounts, the Dark Watchers are described as wearing wide-brimmed hats, reminiscent of styles that might have been common among Spanish settlers or even earlier periods.
- **Staffs or Walking Sticks**: Some witnesses have reported seeing the figures holding staffs or walking sticks, further adding to their mysterious traveler or watcher persona.

- **Behavior and Demeanor**

- **Stillness**: The Dark Watchers are not usually described as actively doing much. They stand still, often in places that would be challenging for a human to reach, such as a steep ridge or mountaintop.
- **Observing**: True to their name, they are often just watching or gazing out into the distance. Their focus could be the horizon, the valleys below, or sometimes, according to unnerved witnesses, the people who spot them.
- **Vanishing Act**: One of the most consistently eerie attributes is their ability to disappear.

They don't typically walk away or move out of sight. Witnesses often describe turning away for a moment or momentarily losing sight of the figure due to an obstacle, and then the Dark Watcher is gone when they look back.

- **Lack of Interaction**: There are rarely, if ever, accounts of the Dark Watchers interacting with those who see them. They don't communicate or acknowledge witnesses; they just observe.

In sum, the Dark Watchers are characterized by their passive, observing nature and their consistent, shadowy appearance. The occasional details of old-world clothing or accessories add to the timeless, eerie quality of the legend. Given the range of descriptions over the years and the inherent mystery surrounding them, they've become an enigmatic staple in the folklore of the region.

Literary References:
   - **John Steinbeck's *Flight***

- **Reference**: In his short story *Flight*, John Steinbeck briefly alludes to the Dark Watchers.

Steinbeck, who was deeply familiar with the landscapes and lore of California, writes:

"Pepe looked up to the top of the next dry withered ridge. He saw a dark form against the sky, a man's figure standing on top of a rock, and he glanced away quickly not to appear curious."

- **Context**: *Flight* tells the story of Pepe, a young man who becomes an inadvertent outlaw and then a fugitive, journeying into the wild terrains of the region. As Pepe travels through the landscape, the brief encounter with the Dark Watcher mirrors the sense of foreboding and the vast unknown that the protagonist confronts.

-Robinson Jeffers and *Such Counsels You Gave To Me*

- **Reference**: Robinson Jeffers, a prominent American poet who lived for much of his life in Big Sur, California, also touches upon the Dark Watchers in his poem *Such Counsels You Gave To Me*. The stanza reads:

"He thought it might be one of the watch-ers,Who are often seen in this length of coast-range,Forms that look human to human eyes,But are certainly not human. They come from behind ridges to watch."

- **Context**: Jeffers was renowned for his deep connection to the rugged landscapes of the Californian coast and frequently intertwined the natural and the mystical in his works. In this poem, the mention of the Watchers, those almost-human entities that come forth to observe, evokes a sense of the sublime—a mix of awe and fear in the face of vast, mysterious nature.

-Literary Impact and Analysis

Both Steinbeck and Jeffers had an intimate knowledge of the California landscape and its associated lore. Their allusions to the Dark Watchers not only acknowledge the legends but also harness the eerie, mysterious essence of these figures to underscore themes of insignificance, the unknown, and man's relationship with nature.

The use of these figures in literature serves to elevate them from mere local myths to symbols that can be employed to evoke specific emotions and themes. When read in the context of their larger works, the Dark Watchers serve as more than just legends; they represent the vast, unknowable mysteries that surround us, the age-old tales rooted in a place, and the eerie feeling of being watched when one thinks they are alone.

It's also noteworthy that literature can amplify local legends, and in the case of the Dark Watchers, mentions by such prominent writers might have helped perpetuate and spread their lore to a wider audience, further embedding them in the collective consciousness.

Theories:

Several theories attempt to explain the phenomenon of the Dark Watchers, though none provide a comprehensive answer:

- **Optical Illusions**: Some believe that the watchers are merely optical illusions. The interplay of light during the twilight hours can create elongated shadows, and the human brain, known for its pattern-recognition tendencies, might interpret these shadows as humanoid figures.

- **Hallucinations**: Factors like fatigue, isolation, and the play of light can sometimes induce hallucinations. Individuals trekking or living in the mountains, under certain conditions, might perceive things that aren't really there.
- **Spiritual Entities**: For those inclined towards the supernatural or metaphysical, the Dark Watchers are sometimes seen as ancient spirits or protectors of the land, watching over the valleys and inhabitants below.
- **Unrecorded History**: Some speculate that these figures might be linked to an unrecorded or forgotten history of the region, where real watchers or guardians once stood sentinel and over time became part of local myth.

Modern Sightings

The allure of the Dark Watchers is intensified by sporadic reports of sightings in recent times. These contemporary accounts often come from hikers, travelers, and locals who are familiar with the landscape yet are left puzzled and unnerved by their experiences. Here's an account from a modern sighting:

A Hiker's Tale

Jenna, an avid hiker from San Luis Obispo, shared her experience from a late afternoon trek in 2015. She was hiking a less-traveled path in the Santa Lucia Mountains, enjoying the solitude and the play of golden light as the sun began its descent.

As she made her way along a ridge, Jenna noticed a figure standing atop a distant peak. Thinking it was another hiker, she continued her trek but couldn't shake off the feeling that something was odd about the lone figure. Its stillness was unsettling. There was no visible movement, no adjusting of a backpack, no taking in the view with hands on hips. Just a stationary, dark silhouette against the backdrop of the setting sun.

Curiosity piqued, Jenna decided to take out her binoculars. Through the enhanced view, the figure appeared even more perplexing. It was undoubtedly humanoid, tall, and draped in what seemed like a flowing garment, perhaps a cloak. There were no discernible facial features—just a shadowy, blank face.

Feeling a mix of excitement and apprehension, she decided to make her way towards the figure, thinking perhaps she'd find a fellow hiker with an interesting tale of why they were standing so still for so long. But as she neared the spot, traversing a dip in the terrain which

momentarily obstructed her view, the figure vanished.
No trace, no footprints, nothing.

Jenna knew the legends of the Dark Watchers, but she had always relegated them to the realm of folklore. However, her personal encounter left her questioning. She hadn't felt threatened, but the encounter had an uncanny quality that stayed with her. When she shared her experience with fellow hikers and locals, she found that she wasn't alone. Others too had their tales, their brief sightings of the shadowy watchers of the Santa Lucia Mountains.

Modern reports like Jenna's are intriguing because they come from individuals who often have no prior inclination to believe in local myths or legends. They're typically rational, grounded in their understanding of the world, yet their experiences challenge their own skepticism.

While no concrete evidence, like photographs or videos, has emerged to substantiate these modern sightings, they continue to be a topic of intrigue and discussion in local communities and among those who trek the trails of the Santa Lucia Mountains. These encounters add a contemporary layer to the age-old tales, ensuring that the legend of the Dark Watchers endures in the modern psyche.

. . .

Conclusion

The Dark Watchers of the Santa Lucia Mountains represent one of those enduring mysteries where myth, history, and natural phenomena intersect. They are a testament to the human spirit's desire to understand, interpret, and at times, marvel at the unknown. Whether they are mere shadows, optical illusions, or something more profound, the Dark Watchers continue to inspire wonder and curiosity in all who hear their story.

Two

THE LADY IN WHITE

LIKE MANY HAUNTED places around the world, the PCT has its own "Lady in White" legend. She's been seen wandering sections of the trail, especially at night, and is believed to be the spirit of a woman who died tragically many years ago.

Origins:

The haunting legend of the Lady in White is not unique to the Pacific Crest Trail (PCT). The specter of a ghostly woman clad in white garments is a recurring motif across the world. To truly understand the origins of the Lady in White on the PCT, we need to explore both the broader cultural framework and the specific history tied to the region.

The archetype of the 'woman in white' can be found in numerous cultures. From the "La Llorona" of Mexican folklore to the "White Lady" legends in the UK, Europe, and parts of Asia, a ghostly female figure often represents sorrow, loss, or tragedy. These spirits are usually tied to traumatic events, often involving betrayal, heartbreak, or untimely deaths.

The Pacific Crest Trail winds through ancient lands that were home to Native American tribes long before European settlers arrived. Many of these tribes had intricate spiritual beliefs, including spirits and ancestors who could influence the living or linger due to unfinished business.

While no direct "Lady in White" figure is prevalent in indigenous legends from the region, it's conceivable that settlers and explorers might have misinterpreted or reframed local spirits or legends in a manner more familiar to their cultural understanding. This amalgamation of indigenous lore with incoming cultural beliefs could have given birth to a new, localized version of the Lady in White.

The era of the American Frontier was a tumultuous period marked by both exploration and conflict. Many tales from this era involve tragedies, and the vast stretches of the PCT were not insulated from these events. Settlers, gold prospectors, and explorers traversed these terrains, and with them came stories of disappearances, hardships, and encounters with the unknown.

Some believe that the PCT's Lady in White might be a settler or the wife or daughter of an explorer or prospector, who met a tragic end in the wilderness. Her continued presence is seen as a manifestation of her unresolved ties to the living world.

Considering the vastness of the PCT and the multiplicity of stories and histories interwoven with its pathways, the origins of the Lady in White could be multifaceted. It's possible that different stretches of the trail have their own versions of this legend, each with its roots in local events or interpretations.

The Lady in White of the PCT is more than just a ghost story; she represents a tapestry of histories, cultures, and beliefs. Her elusive origins remind us of the complexity of narratives and the enduring human need to make sense of the unexplained through stories and legends.

Sightings:

Over the years, numerous hikers have reported encounters with the Lady in White. These sightings usually happen during twilight hours, in the regions of the trail that are more isolated, away from popular camping spots or overlooks.

Most accounts describe her as a silent figure, her white garments flowing as she drifts just above the ground. She never interacts directly with the living but seems to be on a perpetual journey of her own, perhaps retracing her own steps from a past life.

The allure of the Lady in White legend is heightened by reports of sightings and firsthand experiences from those who have journeyed the Pacific Crest Trail. While it's difficult to verify the authenticity of every account (as is the nature of such legends), here's a story that has been passed around in PCT hiker circles for some time:

A Solo Hiker's Encounter- In the summer of 1998, a seasoned hiker named Mark decided to embark on a solo journey across a section of the PCT in Northern California. Having hiked various parts of the trail before, Mark felt confident and was well-prepared for his multi-day trek.

On the third evening, after a day of challenging ascents, Mark decided to set up camp near a clearing that provided a breathtaking view of the valley below. The sun was setting, casting the surroundings in hues of gold and purple, when Mark first noticed a figure at the edge of the clearing.

At first, he assumed it was another hiker. As he squinted, trying to get a clearer look, he realized that the figure was a woman dressed entirely in white. Her dress seemed out of place – not the usual attire one would expect for someone on a rigorous trek. She stood there, unmoving, her gaze fixed on the horizon.

Intrigued and slightly concerned that she might be in trouble, Mark decided to approach her. As he drew closer, a sudden chill in the air made him shudder. The woman's features became clearer: pale, almost translucent skin, and dark eyes that seemed lost in sorrow. She didn't acknowledge Mark's presence.

Feeling an unsettling mix of curiosity and trepidation, Mark mustered the courage to speak. "Hey, are you okay? Do you need help?"

No response. The woman remained still, her focus unwavering.

Thinking it might be best to give her some space and check on her later, Mark returned to his campsite. He prepared his meal, always keeping an eye on the figure. As darkness enveloped the landscape, he noticed she began to fade, almost blending with the encroaching mist.

By the time Mark decided to approach her again, she had vanished entirely. No trace, no footprints, nothing to suggest she'd ever been there.

Disturbed by the encounter, Mark decided to cut his trip short. On his way back, he relayed his experience to a park ranger. The ranger, a local familiar with the stories of the trail, nodded gravely and shared that Mark wasn't the first to encounter the Lady in White.

This story, like many others, is a blend of first-person accounts and the inevitable embellishments that come as tales are retold. Whether Mark's encounter was a product of tiredness, the play of shadows in the twilight, or a genuine paranormal experience is open to interpretation. Yet, such accounts continue to feed into the legend, keeping the mystique of the Lady in White alive for every new generation that steps onto the Pacific Crest Trail.

Like all legends, the tale of the Lady in White is open to interpretation. Some see her as a protective spirit, watching over hikers and ensuring they don't meet the same fate as her. Others view her presence as a cautionary tale, a reminder of the dangers of the trail and the importance of respecting nature.

Local Native American tribes, while acknowledging the presence of spirits and ancestors in the landscape, don't have a direct equivalent to the Lady in White in their lore. However, they respect these stories as part of the ever-evolving relationship between humans and the land.

The legend of the Lady in White adds a layer of mystique to the PCT, reminding hikers that they're not just walking a physical trail but also journeying through a landscape rich in stories, memories, and perhaps, spirits. Whether she's a guardian angel, a lost soul, or just a figment of collective imagination, the Lady in White remains an integral part of the PCT's lore, ensuring that the trail's mysteries endure long after the footprints fade.

Three

MYSTERIOUS LIGHTS

Mᴜsᴛᴇʀɪᴏᴜs ʟɪɢʜᴛs that have been reported by numerous hikers and campers over the years. These lights, often described as orbs or unexplained illuminations, have piqued the curiosity of many and have given rise to a range of theories and legends.

* * *

Theories Behind the Mysterious Lights

- **Atmospheric Phenomena:** Some believe that the lights might be the result of natural atmospheric conditions or optical phenomena, such as ball lightning, St. Elmo's fire, or even reflections from man-made objects.

- **Bioluminescence:** Certain areas along the trail, especially damp and wooded regions, are home to bioluminescent organisms like fungi or insects. The soft glow from these organisms might be mistaken for mysterious lights, especially in the dark.
- **Man-Made Sources:** Some of the lights could be attributed to distant campfires, headlights, or even lanterns from other hikers, seen from vantage points that obscure their origins.
- **Folklore and Legends:** In some parts, these lights are associated with local legends or Native American folklore, often seen as omens or spirits.

-Locations:

Cascade Range in Washington: Some hikers have reported seeing orbs of light floating through the dense forests in the Cascade Range. These lights, often blue or white in hue, are said to move intelligently, weaving through the trees and then disappearing without a trace.

Sierra Nevada Mountains: There are accounts of pulsating lights in the high alpine regions of the Sierra Nevada. These lights, distant and hovering over particular points, have been the subject of much speculation, with some attributing them to reflections off granite surfaces or even distant aircraft.

Near Mount Shasta: Given Mount Shasta's reputation for spiritual and mysterious occurrences, it's no surprise that the areas around it on the PCT also report unusual lights. These lights are often associated with the local legends of the mountain, with some believing them to be spiritual entities or energies connected to the mountain's reputed vortexes.

-Personal Encounters:

One particularly compelling account comes from a thruhiker named David, who, in 2015, recounted his experience near the Oregon-California border. Setting camp for the night, David noticed a series of small, bright lights dancing in the distance. At first, he dismissed them as stars, but their erratic movement soon caught his attention. These lights seemed to hover close to the ground, moving in patterns that ruled out any conventional explanations like aircraft or stars. They lasted for about fifteen minutes before vanishing.

David, being a skeptic, tried finding a logical explanation. He considered the possibility of other hikers with drones or even atmospheric reflections. However, the remote nature of his campsite and the behavior of the lights made these explanations seem unlikely.

The mysterious lights along the PCT, like many unexplained phenomena, remain a blend of natural explanations, personal experiences, and folklore. While some sightings might have simple explanations, others remain enigmatic, adding to the allure and mystique of the trail. For many, these lights are just another facet of the PCT's rich tapestry of experiences, blending the tangible beauty of nature with the intangible mystery of the unknown.

Four

THE PHANTOM PROSPECTOR

Amid the breathtaking vistas, challenging terrains, and deep wilderness of the Pacific Crest Trail (PCT), hikers have often recounted tales of mysterious encounters and eerie sensations. Among these legends, the one that resonates with the historical richness of the American West is the tale of the Old Miner's Spirit, also known as the Phantom Prospector.

The mid-to-late 19th century saw the American West in the throes of gold fever. Thousands flocked to California and its neighboring regions, armed with dreams of striking it rich. The areas surrounding the PCT, especially in California, were no strangers to this fervor, with many trails and regions once buzzing with miners, prospectors, and makeshift gold rush towns.

. . .

The Tale Begins:

The story of the Phantom Prospector is believed to have originated from these gold rush days. As the legend goes, an old miner, often described with a grizzled beard and worn-out clothes, set out on a journey into the depths of the mountains, convinced that he was on the brink of discovering a hidden vein of gold. Some say he was a solitary figure, while others believe he had a family waiting for his return, their hopes pinned on his golden dream.

Despite his determination, the miner never returned. Months turned into years, and while the gold rush era waned, the tale of the missing miner persisted. It's said that he met a tragic fate, perhaps trapped in an underground cave-in, succumbing to the elements, or even facing an altercation with fellow miners over a potential gold discovery.

Sightings on the Trail:

Over the decades, numerous hikers and campers on the PCT have reported sightings of a spectral figure resembling an old miner. These accounts often describe a man, lantern in hand, seemingly searching or digging in the ground. He's seen at dusk or dawn, especially in areas known for historical mining activity.

One particularly poignant account comes from a hiker in the 1980s:

In the twilight hours of a summer evening in the 1980s, a young woman, trekking solo along a remote stretch of the Pacific Crest Trail in Northern California, set up her camp for the night. As the sun's last rays dipped below the horizon, an eerie luminescence caught her attention. From a nearby hill, a faint, otherworldly glow emerged, beckoning her curiosity. Pushing aside her initial apprehension, she decided to investigate. As she drew closer, the silhouette of an old miner materialized from the dimness. Clad in tattered clothes from a bygone era, he seemed deeply engrossed in his task, sifting through the dirt with methodical intent. His lantern, casting a haunting glow, illuminated his immediate surroundings, revealing the specter's singular focus on his endeavor. Tentatively, she called out, hoping to communicate or, at the very least, understand this uncanny presence. Yet, the miner remained undistracted, almost as if he was trapped in his own timeline. As she mustered the courage to approach even closer, hoping for a clearer look, the figure and his ethereal light dissipated leaving no trace.

A second known sighting was in 2005:

Samuel Thompson, an avid outdoor enthusiast, and amateur historian, set out on a solo expedition, aiming to trace some of the old miners' routes that crisscrossed sections of the PCT. He had meticulously planned his journey using old maps and journals. The destination for one of his nights was a now-deserted mining camp-site nestled in a valley that was once a bustling epicenter during the peak of the gold rush.

On the evening in question, after a day of explo-ration, Samuel pitched his tent and, as dusk began to settle, he began recording notes on his findings. The tranquil ambiance of the valley, with crickets chirping and the gentle rustling of leaves, was the perfect backdrop.

It was then that Samuel noticed a dim light emanating from a distance. Assuming it was another hiker or a camper, he didn't pay it much heed. However, as minutes passed, he realized the light was not from a modern flashlight but rather resembled the glow from an old-fashioned lantern.

Curiosity piqued, Samuel decided to investigate. As he got closer, the silhouette of a man became discernible. The figure seemed to be an old man with a slouched posture, wearing ragged clothing typical of 19th-century miners. In one hand, he held the lantern, and in the other, a pickaxe. He seemed deeply engrossed in a task, periodically bending down as if inspecting or searching for something in the ground.

Samuel recounts the air growing noticeably colder as he approached. Taking a deep breath, he called out, "Hello? Can I help you?" To this, there was no verbal response. Instead, the figure slowly raised his head to look at Samuel. His eyes, as Samuel described, "were like deep hollows, filled with years of weariness and an insatiable longing."

Feeling an overwhelming sense of unease, Samuel took a few steps back, but his historian instincts prompted him to take a quick photograph with his camera. Almost immediately after the flash, the spectral miner vanished, leaving behind only the chilling emptiness of the night.

Shaken by the encounter, Samuel barely slept that night. Upon returning from his expedition, he eagerly checked the photograph he had taken. To his disappointment, the image showed only the mining site with the faint glow of the lantern, but no figure.

Samuel shared his experience with the PCT hiker community, reigniting discussions about the Phantom Prospector. While skeptics attributed his experience to fatigue or tricks of the dim light, many believed Samuel had indeed come face-to-face with the elusive spirit.

Regardless of whether one believes in the supernatural, Samuel's detailed account remains one of the most vivid and discussed sightings of the Phantom Prospector on the PCT. It serves as a testament to the trail's rich history and the indelible marks left behind by those who once tread its paths.

Echoes of the Past:

While some believe the Phantom Prospector is the spirit of the old miner, still searching for his elusive gold, others feel his presence is a symbolic representation of the many souls who ventured into the unknown during the gold rush, many of whom faced untold hardships and unfulfilled dreams.

Local historians and enthusiasts have tried to trace the origins of the story, searching for records or accounts of missing miners. However, given the tumultuous and often undocumented nature of the gold rush era, pinpointing a single origin story remains challenging.

Legacy:

The tale of the Phantom Prospector serves as a somber reminder of the sacrifices and risks undertaken by those who ventured westward, driven by ambition and hope. As hikers tread the PCT, stories like these connect them to the rich tapestry of history and human endeavor that has shaped the landscape. Whether the Phantom Prospector is an actual spirit or a legend born from collective memory, his tale adds a layer of mystique to the already enchanting journey along the Pacific Crest Trail.

Five

THE MYSTERIOUS AND BEAUTIFUL MOUNT SHASTA

MOUNT SHASTA, situated in the Cascade Range of Northern California, is one of the most prominent and iconic landmarks of the region. Aesthetically captivating and geologically significant, the mountain's stature in both physical and cultural contexts is profound.

Mount Shasta stands tall at an impressive elevation of approximately 14,179 feet (4,322 meters), making it the fifth-highest peak in California and the second-highest in the Cascade Range.

Mount Shasta is a stratovolcano, composed of alternating layers of solidified lava, volcanic ash, and other volcanic debris. As part of the Pacific Ring of Fire, it's one of the many volcanic peaks in the Pacific Northwest.

The mountain boasts several glaciers, with the

Whitney Glacier being the most prominent. This glacier holds the distinction of being the longest in California.

Mount Shasta has had a tumultuous geological past. It has erupted numerous times over the last 10,000 years, with the most recent significant eruption occurring around 200 years ago. However, minor eruptions and venting have occurred more recently. Geologists consider the volcano dormant, but there is still potential for future eruptions.

The mountain's formation is a tale spanning millions of years. The present-day Mount Shasta is believed to be located on the remnants of an older, now-eroded volcano. Over time, eruptions led to the accumulation of layers, giving the mountain its present-day stature and stratified appearance.

Historical Significance:

- **Indigenous Inhabitants**: Long before European settlers laid their eyes on Mount Shasta, it was a sacred site for indigenous tribes, including the Klamath, Modoc, Shasta, and Ajumawi-Atsugewi. The mountain features in many of their legends and spiritual practices.

- **Exploration Era**: In the early 19th century, Mount Shasta became a focal point for explorers and settlers heading westward. The mountain served as a recognizable landmark for pioneers traversing unfamiliar terrains.
- **Spiritual Movement**: The early 20th century saw a surge in the mountain's spiritual significance with the emergence of New Age beliefs and movements. Mount Shasta became, and continues to be, a pilgrimage site for those seeking spiritual enlightenment.

Mount Shasta's allure isn't just in its towering presence but also in its rich tapestry of geological wonders and cultural significance. As a beacon in the Northern Californian landscape, it continues to inspire, mystify, and captivate those who stand in its magnificent shadow.

The mountain is also shrouded in mystery and legends, let's explore those.

The Native American Legacy and Lore:

Long before modern tales began circulating, the indigenous tribes of the area held Mount Shasta in reverence. The Klamath, Modoc, Shasta, and Ajumawi-Atsugewi tribes all have legends tied to the mountain.

According to Klamath lore, Mount Shasta was inhabited by the spirit chief Skell, the Spirit of the Above-World. Skell and Llao, the spirit chief residing in Mount Mazama (now Crater Lake) in Oregon, once had a fierce battle, hurling rocks and flames, leading to the creation of these natural wonders.

The Hidden City of Lemuria:

The tale of Lemuria, and its supposed hidden city within Mount Shasta, named Telos, is a fascinating blend of ancient legend, New Age beliefs, and modern-day interpretations. Rooted in a combination of historical misunderstanding and mysticism, the story has been embellished and expanded upon for well over a century.

The concept of Lemuria began in the 19th century, not as a mystical city but as a hypothesized lost continent.

- **Geological Theories**: In the 19th century, to explain the presence of similar fossils and geological formations on islands and lands in the Indian and Pacific Oceans, some scientists postulated the existence of a sunken land bridge or continent, which they named "Lemuria." This idea was proposed before the theory of plate tectonics was understood.

- **Esoteric Interpretations**: The Theosophical movement, founded in the late 19th century, integrated the concept of Lemuria into its beliefs. Helena Blavatsky, one of the founders of the Theosophical Society, described Lemuria in her writings as an ancient, lost land that predates even Atlantis. According to her, the Lemurians were an early race of humanity, and their civilization eventually sank due to their spiritual decline.

By the 20th century, the Lemuria legend had found its way to Mount Shasta. Here's how the connection evolved:

- **City of Telos**: New Age enthusiasts began to propagate the belief that when Lemuria sank, its survivors established a hidden city within Mount Shasta called Telos. This subterranean city, they believed, housed the descendants of Lemuria who possessed advanced technologies and vast spiritual knowledge.
- **Lemurian Encounters**: Over the years, several individuals have claimed to encounter Lemurians around Mount Shasta. These beings are often described as tall, with a radiant aura, often wearing white robes.

They're perceived as peaceful, enlightened beings possessing ancient wisdom.

- **Books and Teachings**: Numerous books, channeling sessions, and teachings have emerged detailing the lives and wisdom of the Lemurians in Telos. These accounts describe the city as a complex of tunnels and vast chambers adorned with crystals, advanced technologies, and spiritual centers.

While the idea of a hidden city within Mount Shasta and the existence of Lemurians lacks empirical evidence, the legends persist and continue to attract spiritual seekers, mystics, and curious travelers.

Modern geology and the understanding of plate tectonics have largely debunked the need for a "lost continent" like Lemuria in the Indian or Pacific Oceans. Continents don't simply sink and disappear overnight.

Despite scientific skepticism, the allure of Lemuria and its supposed connection to Mount Shasta persists. The area attracts spiritual retreats, gatherings, and individuals hoping to connect with the energy and wisdom of the ancient Lemurians.

The legend of Lemuria and its hidden city of Telos within Mount Shasta serves as a testament to humanity's fascination with the unknown and the unseen. Whether one views it as pure mythology or a genuine spiritual truth, the tale adds another layer of mystique to the already enigmatic Mount Shasta.

Ascended Masters and the I AM Activity: Spiritual Movements of the 20th Century:

The belief in Ascended Masters and the development of the I AM Activity has deep roots in the esoteric and theosophical traditions of the 20th century. Together, they form a rich tapestry of spiritual teachings and practices that continue to inspire and guide many seekers.

-Ascended Masters: Who Are They?

The idea of Ascended Masters, as we understand them today, has origins in the teachings of the Theosophical Society. Founded in 1875 by Helena Blavatsky, Henry Steel Olcott, and William Quan Judge, the Theosophical Society introduced Western audiences to a synthesis of Eastern and Western spiritual ideas.

Ascended Masters are believed to be spiritually enlightened beings who were once humans but have undergone a series of spiritual transformations. They are thought to have transcended the physical realm and now exist in the higher spiritual planes, guiding humanity's evolution.

Some of the most widely recognized Ascended Masters include Saint Germain, Jesus (often referred to as the

Ascended Master Jesus or the Christ), Kuthumi, El Morya, and many others. These beings have been recognized in various spiritual traditions under different names and roles.

-The I AM Activity: A Modern Revelation

The I AM Activity began in the 1930s with Guy Ballard, who later took on the pen name Godfre Ray King. While hiking on Mount Shasta in California, Ballard claimed to have had a visionary encounter with the Ascended Master Saint Germain. During this meeting, Saint Germain allegedly relayed a series of spiritual teachings to Ballard.

The core teaching of the I AM Activity centers around the "Mighty I AM Presence." This refers to the divine and perfect aspect of an individual, the God-self within every human. By invoking this presence through decrees, affirmations, and meditations, believers can manifest health, prosperity, and spiritual enlightenment.

Ballard, alongside his wife Edna, began disseminating these teachings through books, lectures, and classes. The most well-known of their writings is the "Saint Germain Series," which provides detailed accounts of Guy's experiences and the teachings he received. The couple founded the Saint Germain Foundation, which continues to be the primary organization promoting the I AM Activity.

Over the years, the I AM Activity has faced criticism

and legal challenges. During the late 1930s and early 1940s, there were accusations of mail fraud, which led to a significant court case. However, these allegations were ultimately dismissed.

-Legacy and Influence

The belief in Ascended Masters and the teachings of the I AM Activity has deeply influenced a range of New Age movements, spiritual organizations, and modern esoteric traditions. Even today, the ideas resonate with many spiritual seekers, and both concepts have been integrated or adapted into various contemporary spiritual practices.

In essence, the Ascended Masters and the I AM Activity represent a spiritual framework that emphasizes personal empowerment, divine connection, and the potential for every human to achieve spiritual mastery and enlightenment. Whether approached as symbolic archetypes or genuine spiritual entities, their influence on 20th-century Western spirituality is undeniable.

Mount Shasta's Connection to the Hollow Earth theory and the Enchanted Tunnels:

- **Ancient Tales and Indigenous Beliefs**:
  Before we delve into modern interpretations,

it's essential to recognize that Mount Shasta
was a sacred site for the indigenous tribes in
the region. Native American tribes, like the
Klamath and the Modoc, have their own
legends that speak of hidden caves and
spiritual beings associated with the mountain.

- **Theosophical Influence**: The Theosophical
movement in the late 19th century, which
explored ancient wisdom, spirituality, and
occult sciences, played a role in popularizing
Eastern and esoteric beliefs in the West. Their
discussions about lost continents, like Lemuria
and Atlantis, and Ascended Masters laid a
foundation that would later influence Hollow
Earth theories and tales of subterranean cities.

**-Enchanted Tunnels and the Hollow Earth
Connection**

- **Subterranean Cities**: As New Age and
esoteric beliefs merged with local legends, tales
began to emerge of vast underground cities
and tunnels within Mount Shasta. The most
famous of these is the city of Telos,
purportedly inhabited by the descendants of
Lemurians, an ancient and wise civilization

believed to have taken refuge in the mountain after their continent sank.

- **The Hollow Earth Theory**: This is a concept suggesting that the Earth is entirely hollow or contains substantial interior space. While scientifically discredited, the idea has been a popular topic in folklore, conspiracy theories, and science fiction. Mount Shasta's tales of subterranean realms align with Hollow Earth narratives. Some believe that Mount Shasta contains entrances to these inner realms or that it's a meeting point for extraterrestrials and inner Earth inhabitants.

- **Tales of Encounters**: Over the decades, numerous individuals have reported encounters with mysterious beings around Mount Shasta, believed to be inhabitants of the inner Earth or the lost Lemurian civilization. These beings are often described as tall, dressed in white robes, and emanating wisdom and peace.

- **J.C. Brown Mystery**: In the early 20th century, a story emerged about a British prospector named J.C. Brown who claimed to have discovered a hidden underground city beneath Mount Shasta. He spoke of golden artifacts, mummies, and hieroglyphics. Brown's tale culminated in a 1934 expedition with a group from Stockton, California, to explore the underground city. However, on the day the exploration was set to begin, Brown mysteriously disappeared, and the expedition never took place.

Today, while most geologists and scientists dismiss the Hollow Earth theory and tales of subterranean cities as pure myth, the stories continue to capture imaginations. Mount Shasta remains a spiritual and mystical hotspot, drawing seekers from around the world. The enchanted tunnels, Hollow Earth legends, and stories of ancient civilizations within the mountain contribute to Shasta's rich tapestry of myths and its allure as a place of wonder and mystery.

Mount Shasta's Healing Waters and Energy Vortexes:
The mountain's reputed healing waters and energy vortexes are central to its appeal for many spiritual seekers and mystics.

-Healing Waters:
Throughout history, many cultures have venerated natural springs for their purifying and restorative proper-

ties. At Mount Shasta, there are several springs that are believed by many to possess unique healing qualities.

- **Headwaters of the Sacramento River**: Located at the base of Mount Shasta in the city's park, this spring is easily accessible and is considered a source of pure, healing water by many. Pilgrims often collect water here for spiritual and therapeutic purposes.
- **Stewart Mineral Springs**: Located near Mount Shasta, Stewart Mineral Springs offers bathers the chance to soak in naturally carbonated spring water. Rich in minerals, these waters are said to offer therapeutic benefits. Over the years, countless visitors have claimed rejuvenation and healing after immersing in these waters. The springs also hold spiritual significance for the Native American tribes of the region.

The purity of Mount Shasta's waters is renowned. Snowmelt from the mountain filters down, gathering minerals and energy from the mountain itself. Legends suggest that these waters might even be imbued with the energy of Lemuria or other mystical realms said to be connected with Mount Shasta.

-Energy Vortexes:

An energy vortex is believed to be a location where the Earth's energy spirals and flows in concentrated amounts. Many spiritual believers feel these areas can be used for healing, meditation, and tapping into the deeper realms of consciousness.

Mount Shasta is frequently described as one of the planet's primary chakras or energy centers, likened in importance to other spiritual hotspots such as Sedona in Arizona or Stonehenge in England.

Some esoteric beliefs posit that Mount Shasta represents the Earth's "Root Chakra". In human energetic anatomy, the root chakra is related to fundamental survival and grounding energies. If Mount Shasta indeed represents this chakra on a planetary scale, it might explain the intense grounding and revitalizing energies many visitors report.

Over the years, countless individuals have recounted profound spiritual experiences on the mountain. These range from feelings of deep peace and connectivity to visions and otherworldly encounters. Some of these experiences are attributed to the energy vortexes of Mount Shasta.

Due to its reputation as an energetic hotspot, Mount Shasta attracts many meditation and spiritual retreats.

Participants often report intensified experiences during meditations, from deep insights to energetic healings.

While skeptics might attribute the sensations and reported healings at Mount Shasta to placebo effects or the sheer natural beauty of the mountain, for many, the experiences are undeniably real. Whether it's the rejuvenating waters or the potent energy vortexes, Mount Shasta continues to stand as a beacon for those seeking healing, transformation, and spiritual awakening.

THE WATER MAIDENS OF THE KLAMATH

In the verdant landscapes of Northern California and Southern Oregon, where ancient forests kiss the sky and waterways weave tales older than time, there thrives a legend of ethereal beings – the Water Maidens of the Klamath.

Origins:

The Klamath tribes, like many indigenous peoples, do not view the spiritual and physical realms as separate entities but as intertwined facets of the same reality. This worldview perceives the natural world as teeming with spirits, each with its purpose and domain. The mountains, forests, animals, and, importantly, waters are all imbued with a life force or spirit.

The concept of water spirits, or maidens, is not unique to the Klamath; various indigenous tribes across North America have similar beliefs. However, what distinguishes the Water Maidens of the Klamath is their specific cultural and environmental context.

Water is the essence of life. For the Klamath tribes, whose ancestral lands are graced with an abundance of freshwater sources—from serene lakes to rushing rivers—water is not only a means of sustenance but also a source of spiritual nourishment. These waters, with their reflections of sky, forest, and mountain, serve as mirrors to the cosmos, gateways to the spirit realm.

The creation of the Water Maidens as guardian spirits of these water bodies underscores the tribe's understanding of water's importance. These beings are both protectors and manifestations of water's essence, emphasizing its dual nature: life-giving and, at times, treacherous.

Like most indigenous stories, were passed down orally from one generation to the next. Storytelling in Klamath culture was not mere entertainment. It was a vital means of transmitting knowledge, history, moral lessons, and spiritual beliefs. Through these tales, the younger generation learned about the land, its spirits, and how to live in harmony with nature.

The story of the Water Maidens likely served multiple purposes. It was a reminder of the sanctity of water, a cautionary tale about its unpredictable nature, and a testament to the tribe's spiritual bond with their environment.

As time went on, and the Klamath came into contact with other tribes and later European settlers, their stories, including that of the Water Maidens, may have undergone slight changes. Tales often evolve, influenced by the cultural exchange, adapting while retaining their core essence.

Understanding the origins of the Klamath Water Maidens requires more than just knowing the tale. It demands a deep dive into the tribe's worldview, their reverence for nature, and their age-old traditions of storytelling. These legends, while beautiful on the surface, carry within them the wisdom of ages, the spirit of the land, and the heartbeat of a people who have walked its paths for millennia.

Descriptions and Characteristics:

Often visualized as young, ethereal women with long flowing hair, the Water Maidens are always linked to freshwater sources. They are believed to appear during the twilight hours, casting a silvery glow upon the water's surface, their forms slightly indistinct, as if woven from mist and moonlight. Their voices, melodious and soft, carry songs of ancient times, of love, longing, and the very heartbeat of the Earth.

However, for all their enchanting beauty, the Water Maidens are also beings of duality. They represent both the nurturing and unpredictable facets of nature. It's said that while they might guide a lost traveler or bless an offering left by the water's edge, they can also be capricious, luring the unsuspecting with their songs to watery depths.

Modern Encounters and Tales:

While the tales of the Water Maidens are deeply rooted in Klamath traditions, newer stories and encounters have breathed life into these ancient legends.

Hikers and campers, trekking through the Klamath territories, have occasionally spoken of unexpected encounters. Here's one such recounted tale from a modern traveler:

It was the summer of 1995 when Alex, an avid outdoorsman from Portland, decided to embark on a solo trek across the Klamath territories. He had heard about the legends, of course, but being a man of the modern world, he never put much stock into ancient myths. For him, this journey was about reconnecting with nature and seeking solitude.

One evening, after a particularly grueling hike, he set up camp by a pristine, unnamed lake nestled deep within the forests. As the sun began its descent, casting the world in hues of gold and purple, Alex decided to take a swim. The water, while icy, felt invigorating against his tired muscles.

As dusk deepened, he was jolted from his relaxation by a soft, lilting melody. It seemed to drift from the center of the lake. Perplexed, he looked around, expecting to find another camper or hiker. But he was alone, save for the shimmering reflection of the emerging stars on the lake's surface.

The song grew more pronounced, a melancholic tune that tugged at his heart. Squinting into the dim light, Alex thought he saw the outline of a figure in the middle of the lake—a woman with long, flowing hair, her form bathed in a silvery glow. She seemed to be singing, her voice echoing the haunting melody he heard.

Transfixed, he felt an inexplicable urge to approach her, to join her in the depths. It was as if the song was not just a sound but a call, a beckoning.

It was the sudden hoot of an owl that snapped Alex out of his trance. The vision, or whatever it was, had vanished. The lake was once again just a lake, its waters dark and still under the night sky.

Shaken, he retreated to his tent, his skepticism replaced by wonder. The next day, he related his experience to a local Klamath elder he met along his journey.

The elder, with a knowing nod, simply said, "You've been graced by the Water Maiden. Remember this gift, and treat these lands with respect."

While stories like Alex's are not uncommon among the vast collection of modern encounters in the Klamath region, they always toe the line between the explainable and the mysterious, offering a tantalizing glimpse into the age-old legends that continue to shape the experiences of those who traverse these ancient lands.

Respecting the Maidens:

Regardless of belief, many modern visitors to the Klamath regions approach its waters with a sense of respect and reverence, possibly influenced by the lore of the Water Maidens. It's not uncommon to find small offerings – a flower, a stone, or even a whispered word of thanks – left by the side of a lake or river.

For the Klamath tribes, these practices and tales serve as a bridge to their ancestors, an affirmation of their deep relationship with the land, and a reminder that nature, in all its beauty, remains a force both nurturing and wild.

The Water Maidens of the Klamath stand as luminous figures in the tapestry of North American folklore. They embody the mystery, beauty, and power of nature, serving as a poignant reminder that in every drop of water, there's a story, an echo of times long past, and a hint of the world beyond the veil.

Publisher's Excerpt

CONSPIRACY THEORIES THAT WERE TRUE

THE US PUBLIC HEALTH SERVICE SYPHILIS STUDY IN GUATEMALA

From 1946 to 1948, the U.S. Public Health Service, in collaboration with the Guatemalan government and the

Pan American Sanitary Bureau (a precursor to the Pan American Health Organization), conducted a series of human experiments in Guatemala. These experiments were designed to study the effects and treatment of several sexually transmitted infections, primarily syphilis, but also gonorrhea and chancroid.

ORIGINS:

The U.S. Public Health Service Syphilis Study in Guatemala had its origins in a convergence of medical research interests, the geopolitics of the time, and the readily available vulnerable populations in Guatemala. Let's delve deeper into its origins and the key figures involved:

After World War II, there was heightened interest in understanding and treating sexually transmitted infections (STIs), especially among military personnel. Syphilis was of particular concern because of its widespread prevalence and debilitating effects. The U.S. wanted to test the efficacy of penicillin as a prophylactic against syphilis, and research was directed towards that aim.

The infamous Tuskegee Syphilis Study was already in progress by this time. However, the observational nature of the Tuskegee study (i.e., watching the natural progression of untreated syphilis in already-infected individuals) meant it wasn't suited to testing treatments. A new study was sought, where researchers could deliberately infect subjects and then attempt to cure them.

Guatemala was seen as an advantageous location for such a study due to the existing relationship between the U.S. Public Health Service (USPHS) and the Guatemalan government. There was also a belief (however misguided) that regulations and oversight would be more lenient in Guatemala than in the U.S.

KEY PLAYERS:

- **Dr. John C. Cutler**: A central figure in the Guatemala experiments, Dr. Cutler was a physician with the USPHS. He was directly involved in executing the experiments on the ground in Guatemala. Notably, after the Guatemala study, Cutler would later go on to have a role in the Tuskegee Syphilis Study.

- **Dr. Thomas Parran Jr.**: As the U.S. Surgeon General at the time, Parran was aware of and implicitly approved the Guatemala experiments. He was a vocal advocate for syphilis research and the need to understand and combat the disease.

- **Guatemalan Government Officials**: The Guatemalan government was complicit in the experiments, with various officials, including those in the military and health departments, allowing the study to proceed. Specific figures in the Guatemalan government were collaborators in the project.

- **Pan American Sanitary Bureau (PASB)**: The PASB, a precursor to the Pan American Health Organization (PAHO), played a role in facilitating the experiments. This was part of a broader collaboration between the U.S. and Latin American health services.

The origin and execution of the Guatemala syphilis experiments are indicative of a period when ethical standards for medical research were either not established or not strictly adhered to, but we believe that hasn't changed.

METHODS AND SUBJECTS:

Methods:

- **Intentional Exposure**: One of the most egregious aspects of the experiments was the intentional infection of subjects. The researchers used various methods to achieve this:

- **Direct Inoculation**: Researchers introduced the syphilis-causing bacteria directly to the bodies of subjects. This was often done by making small abrasions on the genitals, face, or arms of the participants and then applying syphilis-infected material to the area.

- **Use of Infected Sex Workers**: Some male subjects were exposed to syphilis by contact with infected commercial sex workers. The researchers had purposefully infected these sex workers with syphilis and then facilitated their contact with subjects.
- **Intraspinal Injections**: In some instances, syphilis-causing bacteria were directly introduced into the spinal fluid of subjects.

- Monitoring and Treatment:

Once infected, subjects were observed for signs and symptoms of the disease. Various interventions were tried, including the use of penicillin, to ascertain its efficacy in preventing or treating the infection. However, not all subjects received adequate treatment.

Many of the participants were neither informed about the nature and purpose of the experiments nor were they aware they were being infected with syphilis or other STIs. Moreover, efforts were made to ensure subjects remained in controlled environments, like prisons or asylums, so they could be easily monitored.

Subjects:

The choice of subjects was deeply problematic, targeting the most vulnerable sections of society who had little or no power to object or provide informed consent.

- **Soldiers**: Members of the Guatemalan military were among the primary subjects. The military setting provided a controlled environment for the researchers.
- **Prisoners**: The confined environment of prisons made inmates a convenient target for these experiments. Both male and female prisoners were subjected to the study, with some male prisoners being exposed to syphilis through contact with infected sex workers.
- **Mental Health Patients**: Institutions housing patients with mental health challenges were also locations for these experiments. The inherent vulnerabilities of these patients, combined with the confined nature of asylums, made them prime targets.
- **Commercial Sex Workers**: Sex workers were both subjects and instruments in the experiments. Many were intentionally infected with syphilis to further the research goals.
- **Orphans**: There is evidence to suggest that children in orphanages were also involved, though the exact extent and nature of their involvement remain less clear than with other groups.

In total, it's estimated that up to 1,500 people were subjected to these experiments. Many never received adequate treatment, and the long-term health consequences for these individuals and their descendants remain largely unquantified.

The methods and choice of subjects used in the Guatemala syphilis study reflect a stark disregard for individual rights, ethics, and basic human decency, making it one of the darkest episodes in the history of medical research.

EXPOSURE:

The U.S. Public Health Service Syphilis Study in Guatemala remained relatively unknown to the public for decades after its conclusion until Dr. Susan Reverby, a Wellesley College historian, came across references to the Guatemala experiment while conducting research on the Tuskegee Syphilis Study. Reverby was sifting through archived papers of Dr. John C. Cutler, one of the primary investigators involved in both the Guatemala and Tuskegee studies.

In her research, Reverby uncovered documents detailing the unethical methods and procedures used in the Guatemala study. Recognizing the significance of her findings, she took it upon herself to delve deeper, resulting in a detailed account of the experiments.

Dr. Reverby initially shared her findings at academic conferences and subsequently published her research. The revelations caused shockwaves in both the medical community and the general public. The immediate reaction was one of horror and disbelief, with many comparing the Guatemala experiments to the Tuskegee Syphilis Study.

Following the exposure, the U.S. government was quick to respond.

In 2010, then U.S. Secretary of State Hillary Clinton and Secretary of Health and Human Services Kathleen Sebelius issued a joint formal apology to the people of Guatemala and to all those affected by the experiments. They condemned the research as unethical and inhumane.

FALLOUT:

In response to the revelations, President Barack Obama ordered the Presidential Commission for the Study of Bioethical Issues to review the Guatemala experiments and ensure that current rules for research participants protect their health and well-being. The Commission's findings reinforced the unethical nature of the study and highlighted areas for improvement in current research ethics.

The Guatemalan government also reacted strongly to the revelations, expressing deep concern and disappointment. The country initiated its own investigation into the experiments to ascertain the full extent of the harm done to its citizens.

As details about the study emerged, it received extensive media coverage, with many outlets highlighting the ethical lapses and comparing the experiments in Guatemala with the infamous Tuskegee study.

The exposure of the Guatemala syphilis experiments serves as a potent reminder of the importance of transparency, oversight, and ethical considerations in medical research. The uncovering of this hidden chapter underscores the value of historical research and the importance of vigilance to ensure such transgressions are not repeated in the future.

But have similar experiments been conducted since? It's a fair question to ask, especially since we're all living in a post-Covid world. We now are confident Covid came from a lab, not from a wet market which we were told was the case. Will we find out decades from now that the entire world were victims to a medical experiment?

* * *

CONSPIRACY THEORIES THAT WERE TRUE

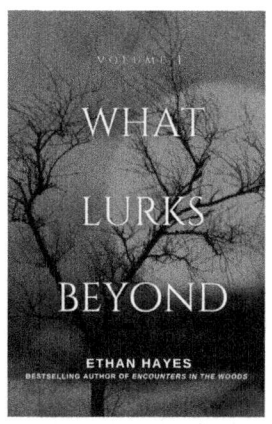

WHITE EYED KID

I know there are many people who are familiar with the legend of the black eyed kids. However, I came across something a little different but similar enough that that's the only thing I can think to compare it to. I wanted to write about this particular encounter more than any other that I've had throughout my life because there is almost nothing at all, even when I search the internet, out there about this particular phenomenon. I know white eyed kids are a phenomenon only because of the maybe five articles I've come across about them in my lifelong search. My encounter happened when I was fourteen years old in the early nineties. This was long before the internet and the initial account of the black eyed kids had been put out there. It was just me and whatever I could find in the local libraries around where I lived at the time. I had always been a sensitive person in that I could sense things that were in my general vicinity when others couldn't and I sometimes even saw physical apparitions. This encounter with the white eyed kids was the most disturbing for many reasons. I used to call the entity I encountered the person with the all white eyes but based on what little information there is out there on this particular phenomenon I know that this entity was one of the white eyed kids. In the interest of saving time I am not going to get into official definitions and parameters of what these entities allegedly do and I am just going to give you what I know for a fact about them. The only thing I know for a fact is what happened during my many encounters with one that started over the summer the year I turned fourteen years old and have continued right up until when I am sitting here typing this all out.

I was visiting a two week long summer camp and a few of my friends were also attending and we all couldn't wait to get there. I had the same friends since I was in kindergarten and we did this every single year. In fact, we all attended two or three camps together over the summer vacation. It was always fun and we were never disappointed except when it was time to leave. Unfortunately where I lived there were no camps that you could go to for the entire summer. There were several summer camps in the area though because where I grew up there were woods everywhere. It wasn't uncommon for the woods in the area to be where our parents would find my friends and I when we would be late in getting home for supper or when we otherwise just needed a break from everything. The woods were our comfort and solace and even despite the terrifying things I've seen within them throughout my life, even up until that point, they still brought me comfort and the same was true for my friends. This was the second camp my friends and I would be attending that summer. The other one was for two weeks and so was this one and there was a one week break in between the two. My friends and I couldn't wait to get back to hanging out and having fun.

There was swimming in the lake and despite having our own cabins, there were nights when we would have the option of camping out in tents if we wanted to. Normally my two best friends and I stayed in the cabin and hung out. Most of the other girls liked to go and camp in the tents on those nights but we stayed behind to have the whole place to ourselves. Not that it really mattered, we always got along well with everyone else who attended, for the most part.

My two best friends are Kate and Gretchen and they are the two who I would always be attending the summer camps with. We were practically all joined at the hip at all times and so it was unusual for one of us to be seen without the other two. On the night of my first encounter Kate, Gretchen and I had the cabin to ourselves. There were two counselors who stayed with us but they were out helping with the camping festivities. We really weren't doing anything bad but we just liked the idea of having the entire place to ourselves. The cabins were fairly large and we were young. It felt like freedom I guess, you know how it is at that age. The counselors sometimes wouldn't come back at all and when they did it would be in the middle of the night. On the night of the encounter they hadn't returned by the time midnight rolled around and we decided to go to bed. Now, before I explain what happened let me just tell you a little about how the cabins were set up. There were six girls and two counselors in each cabin. There were four sets of bunk beds but the counselor's bunks were in a separate back room. I was on the bottom bunk in the main room and Gretchen was staying on the top of that bunk. Kate was on the top of the bunk right next to us.

The camp had its own security and was really out of the way and so there was no reason, not really, to have any locks on the doors. That's why it was so strange when we woke up at around three o'clock in the morning to someone banging on the door. My senses were immediately on full alert and my mind was racing. Kate hadn't even seemed to have heard the knocking and Gretchen jumped up as well. She immediately wondered out loud why someone would be knocking. Not only was it obnoxiously loud but the counselors knew that they could just walk in. I was scared right away but decided that since I was the one on the bottom bunk I should get up and go see who was there. It had to have been the counselors or at least one of them but it made no sense why they would purposely knock just to wake us up. Unless, maybe they were playing some sort of prank on us. We all pranked each other often, even the counselors, so that wouldn't have really been anything new. I calmed down and realized that's probably what was going on. I went to the door and flung it open and once I did I jumped out and yelled "gotcha!" There was no one there though. Gretchen whispered from behind me where she was still cuddled up in her bunk and asked me who it was. I told her there seemed to be no one there and we were both pretty sure that someone was trying to scare us. I was annoyed more than anything else and decided to give whoever it was a taste of their own medicine. I saw movement in the trees about ten feet in front of the door to the cabin and so I walked right to it. I couldn't see who or what it was but it looked like long, blonde hair like that of one of the counselors who had been assigned to our cabin. Her name was Carly and I really thought that it was her. It looked like someone had tried to run without being seen from behind one tree to another but I could still see the hair somehow. I asked Gretchen if she wanted to come with me and she said no. I put my sneakers on which were right next to the door and confidently walked outside to try and scare Carly before she got to scare me. This was all very typical and I was no longer even thinking anything of it. I don't think Gretchen was either because she laid back down and closed her eyes to go back to sleep. Kate still had barely even moved.

I could see the blonde piece of hair behind the tree until I literally blinked and it was gone. I thought maybe she had just moved a little bit so she couldn't be seen. I got to that tree and jumped out again, trying to scare her. There was no one there. Now, I was scared and just wanted to get back into the cabin and curl up in my bed. However, before I could do that I heard someone say my name. It was a female voice and somehow I could tell that it was close and coming from just a little further ahead. The voice sounded like that of a girl much younger than anyone who would be attending this camp. This camp was for young people in the sixth, seventh and eighth grades. Essentially it was only for middle school kids. The voice that had called out to me sounded like that of an eight or nine year old child. I was freaked out and annoyed but decided to follow the sound and see who it was once and for all. I walked about twenty more feet into the woods and then heard someone say my name again. It was the same voice only louder this time. I turned to my left and saw a teenage girl standing there.

She had very pale blonde hair, almost to the point where it was white. She wasn't dressed for the nice weather and had on a heavy and bulky looking black hooded sweatshirt and green sweatpants. It was a mild and humid night and I immediately wondered how she wasn't hot. That thought left my brain immediately when she said my name again but was able to do so without moving her mouth. This was telepathy but I wasn't aware of what that was back then. The paranormal and extraterrestrial fields weren't as in the public eye or as widely known as they are today back in the early nineties. It felt to me like my name was being somehow beamed into my head in order for me to hear it. I knew immediately though that this was the same person who had been calling out to me all along and more than likely she was the one who had banged on the door to the cabin and woken us all up. I asked her who she was and what she wanted. She replied that I didn't have to speak out loud and that all I had to do was think my questions and thoughts and she would hear me. I know most people think they would be so terrified by this point, especially back then. They'd think that they wouldn't want to stay and carry on a conversation with this strange and unknown person in the woods. I understand that and a part of me did want to just turn and run but this entity came with a sense of peace and calm that's unlike anything I had ever felt before or even since, except for when in her presence. She wanted me to feel comfortable. I immediately noticed that her eyes were all white. They were white like the whites on my eyes except there was absolutely no color to them at all. Her skin was very pale but none of this scared me at the time. I quickly realized I couldn't move. I had tried to advance on the girl but couldn't. When the thought crossed my mind to approach her she telepathically said, "don't" and held out one of her arms. She looked like she was about nineteen years old, give or take a year or two. She was as tall as me and that last word she said to me was said in a very demanding tone. Up until this point she had sounded childlike and playful. Not anymore.

She told me to stay where I was and that I was going to do something for her. When I thought I didn't want to do anything for her she replied that whether I wanted to or not, that's what I was going to do. Suddenly I was dizzy and the last thing that I remember before I woke up back in my bed in the cabin was something like little beams of bright light coming out of her eyes and beaming into my eyes. It was like I was being entranced or something. I couldn't blink and I still couldn't move. I jumped up and was immediately terrified. I looked around and saw that Kate was asleep in the top bunk next to me and Gretchen was coming out of the bathroom. I was in a full blown panic. She didn't ask about the night before or what had happened when I went into the woods- nothing at all. I asked how I had gotten back into my bed and she looked at me like I was insane. She said I must've been dreaming because no one had knocked on the door and my entire memory of what happened once the knock came and after that, before I left the cabin, had belonged only to me. Gretchen remembered falling asleep and staying that way through the entire night. My sneakers were in the exact same spot they always were and nothing else out of the ordinary seemed to have been happening. I became convinced that I had merely had an extremely vivid dream. I told Gretchen and Kate about it later on that day and they both said it sounded cool and that it was probably just a really strong dream that only FELT very real. I knew in my mind that this wasn't the case but wanted so badly for them to be right that I allowed them to help me convince myself that it was all nothing but a strange dream. I never felt right or the same while in the woods again but I did continue to spend time camping and hiking and continued to attend multiple summer camps every summer until I turned eighteen. Then I became a counselor for a few years and worked at almost all of the camps I had always attended.

Throughout the years I have had several dreams like the one I thought that I had that night. I would only have those types of dreams when I was sleeping in the woods, whether in a tent or otherwise. Somehow I was always lured out of sleep and bed and into the woods to the sound of the same girl calling my name. Years went by and these strange and very vivid dreams continued. I grew up but the girl who I had become accustomed to meeting in the middle of the night in the woods in my dreams never did. She always stayed the same and she always wore the exact same outfit. I didn't know what to make of it and it wasn't until about fifteen years after that very first encounter that I started to understand that I hadn't been dreaming at all. I had been chosen but for what I still really don't know. I've tried to have hypnotic regressions done but I always end up with extreme migraine headaches and terrible nosebleeds. There is something blocking my memories of what happens after the girl shoots those lights out of her own eyes and into mine. I've uncovered just a little bit more and I'll tell you about what those other details are, just be warned they're strange, make no sense and scarce.

I started having random memories of running through the woods and coming to a giant light beam. I walk into the light beam which is coming from what I somehow just know to be a cloaked UFO and the light floats me up into the ship. The girl is always next to me when I stop running, somehow, but she is never running along with me or anything. She simply appears whenever I stop. If I would get tired of running and I would stop to catch my breath, she would appear next to me and order me, albeit gently, to keep going until I made it to the ship. Sometimes she would tell me I had to make it to the light and sometimes she would say the ship. From the very first encounter with her I somehow always knew what she meant. I believe this to be because she shows me the image of it in my mind by using the same telepathy we always used to speak to each other. I have vague memories of being on some sort of futuristic looking ship that looks straight out of the new Star Wars movies. All of my memories of being on those ships have me attending what seem to me to be some sort of grand reunions with all sorts of creatures and beings I somehow know in the moment but whom I definitely have no clue who or what they are at any other time. I am comfortable and feel more at home than in my own house with my human family when I am hugging and greeting these otherworldly beings. I swear that once I saw Bigfoot and several other human beings who I hadn't ever met before but who seemed to be overseeing the whole thing from a bit of a distance on the other side of the room.

The walls are perfectly round with no sharp edges. Everything is extremely sterile and the colors are mostly white and metallic gray. The ship itself is glossy and black on the outside. It's like a black mirror. I don't have many more memories of being in the ship except a little room the size of a cell where I have some memories of sleeping in a small bed. I can see the Earth from the tiny window in that little room. I am never fearful. As far as the white eyed girl, there are more of her I'm sure of it. The only thing that I have ever come across about the so-called white eyed kids phenomenon is that people almost always come across them when out in the woods. They are almost always alone and they speak telepathically. The person who they choose to communicate with always feels as though they had been compelled to do something through some sort of telepathic conversation where they were given instructions but they're never able to remember it. The girl was very soft spoken, but firm when she had to be. Once I had a memory of trying to resist her and I ended up on the ground with searing pain as though I were having an actual heart attack. She had reached her hand out and made a squeezing motion with her fist. I believe she was squeezing my heart and threatening me that I would die if I didn't comply. I just don't have full memories and I don't really know what it's all about.

I wish I had more information for you but I don't. I can send you more encounter stories about a lot of other things I've seen and come across throughout my life. It's been happening to me ever since I was very little. I've often wondered if the ability to see and sense, and sometimes communicate with, spirits is the reason for the interactions with the white eyed girl. Is she an extraterrestrial messenger of some sorts? Is she a recruiter? Is she something altogether different that we as human beings can't even begin to fathom or understand yet? Who or what are the entities I am constantly greeting while up in the ship and why am I always made to think it was all some sort of dream? I always wake up right back in my bed with nothing amiss and everything in its place. I have even tried living in a place in the middle of a city with no woods around but it didn't matter. I would always be instructed to find the ship. Maybe this is why I've always been drawn to the woods in the first place. Maybe it's because they need to have easy access to me, for whatever reason. It could also be, and I'm pretty sure this is what it is, that they have had me tagged since birth and I serve some purpose for them that I'm not meant to understand, not yet anyway. One more thing I'd like to say is that I cannot find one single other encounter where the person remembers anything more than the first initial encounter with the white eyed kid in the woods. They usually remember some sort of telepathy happening but that seems to be the extent of it. I really hope this phenomenon takes off and gets the attention it very much deserves as I am sure there are thousands if not millions of others out there just like me. These white eyed kids don't seem to be connected to the black eyed kids legend in any way, shape or form and yet they're being lumped in with them. I've done just as much research on the BEK phenomenon hoping to find some sort of connection since there is so much more information on the latter entity. I just can't put them together though or see how they're connected. They each have solid eyes, either black or white, which technically are neither actual colors. That's it for now and I really hope this will encourage people with similar experiences, even if only a slight bit of memory remains, to come forward so maybe we could all stop living in fear and suffering in silence.

WHAT LURKS BEYOND

STRANGE NATIONAL PARK DISAPPEARANCES:
VOLUME 2

THE MYSTERY OF JACOB GRAY

On a brisk morning in early April 2017, the quiet streets of
Port Townsend, Washington, witnessed the departure of
22-year-old Jacob Gray. Laden with camping gear and

fueled by a sense of adventure, Jacob set out alone on his bicycle, towing a trailer behind him. His destination: the rugged wilderness of Olympic National Park's Daniel J. Evans Wilderness.

The following day, April 6, the serene landscape of Sol Duc Hot Springs Road, known among the Quileute Indians for its 'sparkling waters', harbored a perplexing scene. Jacob's bike and trailer, still laden with most of his gear, were found abandoned about six and a half miles up the road. Adding to the mystery, four arrows were discovered planted in the ground, with another protruding from the back of the trailer. Nearby, a bow lay discarded, as if hastily dropped. Yet, there was no sign of Jacob.

Ranger John Bowie, upon inspecting the scene that afternoon, was met with more questions than answers. Could the cyclist have ventured to the river for water? The icy waters of the Sol Duc, he knew, were merciless to the unprepared. Or had Jacob hitched a ride to the nearby hot springs? The scene puzzled Bowie, an unsettling tableau amidst the wilderness.

The following day, Ranger Bowie enlisted his colleague, Brian Wray, to re-examine the area. Wray found the bike and trailer undisturbed on April 8, as if frozen in time since their discovery.

As days stretched into a year, the mystery of Jacob Gray deepened. How had he traveled from the site of his abandoned bike to a ridge above Hoh Lake, over 5,300 feet above sea level and at least fifteen miles away? The condition of the bike and trailer, intact and fully equipped, offered no clues. A thorough check at the Sol Duc Hot Springs Resort yielded nothing; the rangers speculated that Jacob might have fallen into the river, planning to search once the waters receded.

On April 7, Ranger Wray unearthed a list of telephone numbers among Jacob's belongings. He contacted Jacob's sister, Mallory, who urged him to inform their parents in Santa Cruz. A family inventory revealed that a water filter and a Camelbak backpack were missing from the trailer.

The search for Jacob Gray was now in full swing. The Clallam County Sheriff's Office deployed teams and dogs, but their efforts bore no fruit. Olympic Mountain Rescue volunteers, scouring the area on April 12, found a telling trace: a mossy rock, evidence of a switch from hiking to running shoes, leading to the river's edge. Signs of a slip and fall into the river, and possible exit further downstream, heightened the sense of urgency.

By April 13, the grim reality set in: the searchers were likely looking for a body, not a survivor. Cadaver dogs indicated a possible corpse beneath a logjam, yet exhaustive searches along the river yielded nothing.

The search, now limited but continuous, carried on in Olympic National Park. Despite the availability of volunteer dog teams and resources, the park's approach was selective, focusing on specific areas and rejecting additional volunteer assistance.

Jacob's fate remained a mystery until August 10, 2018, when a team of biologists, studying marmots in the mountains, stumbled upon a tragic discovery. Jacob's remains, along with his clothes, wallet, and additional gear, were found in a remote area above Hoh Lake, far from where he had left his bike.

The location, likely prone to avalanches in April, was off any marked trail. The skeletal remains were visible from the air, lying exposed on a treeless ridge. The trek from Sol Duc to Hoh Lake, through dense forests and alpine slopes, was a challenging ten-mile journey, culminating at an altitude of 5,300 feet.

The following morning, police discovered more clothing near the remains. Olympic National Park spokesperson Penny Wagner confirmed that the clothing matched what Jacob's family expected him to wear. The King County Medical Examiner's Office, using dental records, confirmed the identity of the remains. No signs of foul play were evident at the scene, which bore no resemblance to a campsite.

Jacob's father, Randy Gray, had held onto hope, imagining his son alive and well, perhaps fishing or working elsewhere. An avid outdoorsman, Jacob had a penchant for solitary camping trips. Randy had searched relentlessly for his son, extending his efforts beyond the Sol Duc Valley to other parts of the country and Canada.

The official cause of death, determined by Clallam County Deputy Coroner Christi Wojnowski, remained inconclusive. An autopsy was impossible, but the lack of trauma and the presence of essential survival gear led authorities to believe hypothermia was the cause.

Yet, questions lingered in the wake of this tragic discovery. Why had Jacob, who planned to head east, inexplicably turned west without telling anyone? What prompted him to leave his bike and gear so visibly unsecured? The significance of the arrows remained an enigma. And crucially, how did he traverse fifteen miles through snow to reach such a high altitude? Was his intention in the wilderness one of despair, or was it simply a tragic turn of fate?

In the end, Jacob Gray's story, woven into the tapestry of the Olympic National Park's rugged landscape, remains shrouded in mystery, the answers carried away with him into the silence of the mountains.

* * *

STRANGE NATIONAL PARK DISAPPEARANCES: VOLUME 2

Seven

THE SIERRA SOUNDS & BIGFOOT / SASQUATCH

IN THE EARLY 1970S, amidst the densely forested and rugged landscape of the Sierra Nevada mountains, a series of eerie and anomalous vocalizations were captured, forever intriguing and baffling those who seek the truths hidden within the American wilderness. These vocalizations, popularly known as the "Sierra Sounds," are among the most debated and analyzed pieces of audio evidence associated with the Bigfoot phenomenon. Central to this story is Ron Morehead, an adventurer and researcher, whose fortuitous presence at a remote hunting camp led to the capturing of these enigmatic sounds.

-The Beginning: An Unexpected Discovery

Ron Morehead and Al Berry, the latter a journalist, along with other companions, were regulars at a hunters' camp situated in a particularly isolated region of the Sierra Nevada mountains. The camp's remoteness required them to use mules or hike several miles to reach it.

On one of their trips in the early '70s, the group began to experience a series of unusual events. They heard strange, guttural vocalizations echoing through the dense forest, footsteps around their camp at night, and even found what appeared to be large bipedal footprints. Intrigued and somewhat unnerved, they decided to set up recording equipment to capture these sounds.

The recordings they captured over various trips were nothing short of astonishing. The vocalizations ranged from high-pitched chatters to deep, resonant growls, and even what sounded like a language – a rapid series of clicks, grunts, and whistles, which bore no resemblance to any known animal or human sounds.

Morehead and Berry weren't the only ones to experience these phenomena. On several occasions, other hunters and guests at the camp reported similar encounters, reinforcing the notion that the sounds weren't merely the result of some elaborate hoax.

-Analysis and Scrutiny

Recognizing the potential importance of these recordings, Morehead and Berry sought expert analysis. Dr. R. Lynn Kirlin, an electrical engineer with expertise in sound, and later, Scott Nelson, a retired Navy crypto-linguist, both analyzed the sounds. Kirlin's primary focus was on the unique pitch and frequency, noting that the vocal range was broader than that of humans. Nelson, on the other hand, delved into the possibility that the sounds could represent a structured language, suggesting that the speed and complexity of the sounds pointed towards a genuine form of communication.

As with most pieces of evidence in the realm of crypto-zoology, the Sierra Sounds have faced their share of skepticism. Detractors argue that the sounds could be manipulated or produced by known animals or even humans skilled in mimicry. Yet, the conditions under which the sounds were recorded, coupled with the corroborating experiences of different individuals, make it a challenging case to dismiss outright.

Ron Morehead, throughout the years, has remained a central figure in bringing these sounds to public consciousness. He has written about the experiences, given numerous interviews, and even produced CDs of the Sierra Sounds. More than just audio clips, for Morehead, they represent a deeper connection with the mysteries that our natural world still harbors.

The Sierra Sounds, as popularized by Ron Morehead and Al Berry, stand as a tantalizing piece of auditory evidence in the Bigfoot enigma. Whether one sees them as irrefutable proof of an undiscovered creature or merely anomalies open to interpretation, they undeniably add a fascinating chapter to the ongoing quest to understand the mysteries of the great American wilderness.

Bigfoot / Sasquatch:

The name "Sasquatch" is an Anglicized derivative of the word "Sésquac," which means "wild man" in a Salish Native American language. Long before Europeans set foot on North American soil, indigenous tribes from California to the Pacific Northwest had tales of large, hairy, bipedal creatures that lived deep in the woods. These creatures were, in many stories, seen as spirits or protectors of the woods, possessing supernatural abilities to blend into their surroundings or vanish into thin air.

The modern fascination with Bigfoot began mainly in the mid-20th century, especially after a series of footprint casts were discovered in California in the 1950s. Since then, sightings have been reported across North America, from the swamps of Florida to the snowy peaks of the Rocky Mountains. But the dense forests of the Pacific Northwest, including those the PCT traverses, remain a significant hotspot for Bigfoot reports.

Those who claim to have seen Bigfoot often describe it as standing between 7 to 10 feet tall, covered in dark brown or reddish hair, and having a distinctive foul odor. Its eyes, when caught in the beam of a flashlight or lantern, are said to glow red or yellow. Contrary to the menacing portrayal in some media, many reports suggest Bigfoot is more curious than aggressive, often watching from a distance or trying to avoid human interaction.

-An Encounter with Sasquatch:

This is a true story from my past, an experience that has stayed with me for over 20 years. As someone who loves backpacking and has explored remote areas in the western states, encountering various wildlife, including grizzly bears, I had never encountered anything as strange as what happened on this particular occasion.

It was late summer 1989, a Friday evening after work. I decided to venture out alone, accompanied by my dogs. My destination was White Rock Lake in Tahoe National Forest, a place I had never been to before. The challenge was finding the lake since the roads were unmarked. According to the topo map, I could reach it via a 4-wheel drive road.

I found myself driving slowly on rough, rocky dirt roads, trying to figure out my location. The roads seemed to fade away or intersect with other 4-wheel drive paths, leaving me disoriented. I was in the middle of nowhere, with no lakes, significant creeks, or clear destinations in sight for miles.

Deciding to wait until daylight to avoid further confusion in the darkness, I pulled my 4-wheel drive pickup off the road, although I probably didn't need to since I hadn't seen anyone or anything. I parked a few yards away from the rocky road, hidden by the surrounding trees. I grabbed my sleeping bag and laid it out in front of my truck, settling down with my dogs under the starry night sky.

Sometime in the early morning, around 3 or 4 a.m., while it was still pitch black, I woke up to the sound of something walking towards me on the road. It was a heavy, steady footfall, clearly bipedal in nature. At first, I assumed it might be another backpacker, given the rhythm of the steps. But then I questioned why someone would be out here on this road in the middle of the night, without light, surrounded by miles of dense forest. Although I knew it wasn't a bear (I had encountered many bears in the wild), I couldn't identify what it could be. Nonetheless, I still thought a back-packer was the most reasonable explanation.

As the sound grew closer, I pondered whether I should say something, but I didn't want to startle anyone unnecessarily. I convinced myself that the passerby would simply continue on without noticing me. However, my growing nervousness was unusual, as there aren't many things in the wilderness that make me feel that way. Strangely, my dogs remained silent and motionless, which added to the suspense. Typically, they would have at least barked as a warning. This heavy bipedal entity continued approaching, getting closer to the spot where I had parked my truck off the road. I lay there, holding my breath. I didn't know what to expect and hoped it would pass by without even realizing I was there. The darkness obscured my vision completely.

As it drew nearer, I could sense its size, as the rhythm of its footsteps indicated a significant presence. In my nervousness, I remained utterly silent. At that moment, a thought of encountering a sasquatch didn't cross my mind. I had never given much thought to such things, especially in the Sierras. But that was about to change. The entity reached the point where my truck was parked off the road... and suddenly, silence. It stopped. Although I couldn't see it in the darkness, it stood only a few yards away from where I lay in my sleeping bag.

I'm not sure if I made a sound or if one of my dogs did, but something triggered a reaction from it. The entity emitted the most horrifying, piercing scream imaginable—a scream that defies description. It had lungs like nothing I had ever encountered before. Then, still screaming, it turned around and ran back down the road in the darkness at an astonishing speed. It continued to scream, the sound echoing through the forest without ceasing. I could hear the screams fading in the distance.

I lay there in complete shock, unable to believe what had just transpired. Eventually, I snapped out of it and quickly gathered my belongings, tossing them into my truck. My dogs were equally disturbed by the experience. I assumed the entity had moved far away by then, so before leaving the area, I drove down the road with my brights on, attempting to find any footprints or signs of something unusual. My adrenaline was pumping. Although I didn't actually step out of the truck, I opened the door and peered down, hoping to spot footprints or any clue about what I had encountered. The road was too rocky to show any prints. I then let my dogs out, hoping they might pick up a scent (although I didn't know what I would do if they did), but strangely, they immediately jumped back into the truck. This was out of character for them. I tried once more, but they insisted on staying inside. Realizing they were as unnerved as I was, I knew it was time to get out of there. I drove several miles back toward the main road, my adrenaline still surging.

Before this experience, I hadn't given much thought to sasquatches, but now I'm definitely a believer. People try to explain it away, but I know what I heard. I didn't see anything, nor did I detect any unusual odor, but it was so close that I could feel its presence. And when it screamed, it was so close that I'm surprised I didn't feel the spit from its mouth. Nothing in those forests could scream like that or run that fast, especially nothing walking upright. I don't dwell on the subject of sasquatch, nor have I made it my mission to search for them, but I know they exist. My experience is still vivid in my mind. Whether or not others believe it is irrelevant to me. I'm not sharing this account to convince anyone; I'm simply sharing an experience I had one night in the Sierras near Truckee.

Of course, for every believer, there's a skeptic. Critics argue that many Bigfoot sightings are merely misidentifications of known wildlife, hoaxes, or the products of overactive imaginations. The blurry photos and grainy videos that occasionally surface are often debunked or remain inconclusive.

Yet, many dedicated researchers and enthusiasts continue their quest for definitive evidence. They point to the sheer number of consistent reports from unrelated individuals over the decades as indicative of something genuine lurking in the forests.

Whether Sasquatch is a real undiscovered species, a legend passed down through generations, or a blend of truths and misinterpretations, it remains an enduring symbol of the wild unknowns that the PCT represents.

TULE LAKE: HISTORY, SUFFERING, AND THE PCT

TULE LAKE, located near the California-Oregon border, is not just another natural wonder one might encounter on a long journey. This site bears the weight of a painful chapter in American history and the unspoken narratives of those unjustly imprisoned.

Origins of the Tule Lake Internment Camp:
   -Prelude to Internment:
The origins of the Tule Lake Internment Camp can be traced back to the growing tensions between the United States and Japan in the years leading up to World War II. Japan's imperial ambitions in East Asia clashed with American interests in the region, resulting in economic sanc-

tions and diplomatic confrontations between the two countries.

-Attack on Pearl Harbor and Its Immediate Aftermath:

The attack on Pearl Harbor on December 7, 1941, by Japanese forces, dramatically intensified anti-Japanese sentiments in the U.S. Amidst the shock and anger, suspicion towards Japanese Americans grew, both those who were immigrants (Issei) and their American-born children (Nisei). Despite no evidence of espionage or sabotage from the Japanese American community, public and political opinion began to shift towards the idea of mass internment.

On February 19, 1942, President Franklin D. Roosevelt signed Executive Order 9066. This order authorized the U.S. military to designate areas from which "any or all persons may be excluded." While the order didn't specify a particular ethnic or racial group, it was primarily used to forcibly relocate Japanese Americans from the West Coast to internment camps.

-Tule Lake's Establishment:

Of the ten internment camps established, Tule Lake was one of the first, opened in May 1942. It is located near Newell in northern California, on what was then reclaimed marshland. The site was chosen because it was remote, far from major population centers, and had a railway connection for easy transport of internees.

Originally, Tule Lake was similar to other internment camps. However, in 1943, the U.S. government issued a controversial "loyalty questionnaire" to Japanese Americans over the age of 17. Those who answered in ways deemed "disloyal" to the U.S. (such as refusing to forswear allegiance to the Japanese Emperor, a confusing question for many since they had no prior allegiance to the Emperor to begin with) were sent to Tule Lake, which was transformed into a high-security segregation center. Consequently, Tule Lake became the largest and most controversial of the camps, housing those deemed "disloyal" and subjected to stricter security measures. At its peak, the camp held around 18,000 people, making it the largest of the ten internment camps.

-Surrounding Conditions and Challenges:

The conditions at Tule Lake were harsh. Set against a backdrop of a barren landscape, the camp suffered from dust storms in summer and intense cold in winter. The barracks were cramped, and the constant surveillance from guard towers and military police was oppressive.

-End of Internment:

The internment of Japanese Americans was finally ended in 1945, though many of the internees had lost their homes, businesses, and possessions. Tule Lake officially closed on March 20, 1946.

In the subsequent years and decades, the internment of Japanese Americans during World War II has been recognized as a grave injustice. In 1988, President Ronald Reagan signed the Civil Liberties Act, formally apologizing for the internment and providing reparations to surviving Japanese American internees.

The story of Tule Lake and the broader internment experience serves as a potent reminder of the dangers of wartime hysteria and the erosion of civil liberties in the name of national security.

Ghosts of Tule Lake:

Like many sites of suffering and trauma, Tule Lake has its share of haunting tales. Some have reported ghostly apparitions in the areas surrounding the camp, which they believe to be the restless spirits of former internees. These spirits are said to wander the periphery of their former prison, trapped in the echoes of their unresolved past.

One tale speaks of a sorrowful woman in traditional Japanese garb, seen wandering near the remains of the barracks. Another account tells of soft, haunting lullabies heard on still nights, possibly sung by mothers who were interned there, trying to comfort their children in the cold, unforgiving environment.

Visitors and researchers, spending nights near the camp, have reported feelings of being watched or an inexplicable sadness pervading the area. These might not be ghostly encounters in the conventional sense, but they certainly underscore the intense emotional resonance of the place.

Connection to the Pacific Crest Trail:

While the Pacific Crest Trail doesn't directly pass through the Tule Lake Internment Camp, its proximity means that hikers on certain stretches of the trail could easily make a detour to visit this historic site. The trail provides a connection, a pathway through history and nature that prompts reflection on humanity's capacity for both beauty and cruelty.

Tule Lake and its haunting tales serve as a stark contrast to the natural beauty of the PCT. It's a reminder that while nature can heal, history, especially when unacknowledged or forgotten, can continue to inflict wounds.

Today, the Tule Lake Segregation Center is a National Historic Landmark, ensuring that the stories of those who were imprisoned there will never be forgotten. The ghost stories, whether based in fact or the product of emotional responses to the camp's painful history, reinforce the importance of remembering and understanding this dark chapter in American history.

For those hiking the Pacific Crest Trail, a visit to Tule Lake offers a moment of somber reflection, a chance to pay respects, and an opportunity to learn from the past.

Nine

TAHOE TESSIE - THE SERPENT OF SIERRA NEVADA

NESTLED amidst the towering peaks of the Sierra Nevada lies the crystal-clear waters of Lake Tahoe. Known for its stunning beauty, recreational activities, and rich history, the lake also harbors a deeper mystery, one that has captivated locals and visitors for decades - the legend of Tahoe Tessie.

* * *

Origins:

The tales of a large, serpentine creature residing in the depths of Lake Tahoe date back several centuries, with the region's indigenous people, the Washoe and Paiute tribes, already having stories of a mysterious water creature. These tales describe a creature that would emerge at dusk, its scales reflecting the setting sun, leaving an otherworldly glow on the water's surface.

Modern sightings began to gain traction in the 1950s and 1960s, as tourism in the Lake Tahoe region flourished. The creature was affectionately dubbed "Tahoe Tessie," drawing comparisons to Scotland's famous Loch Ness Monster. As the tales spread, so did the intrigue, with Tessie becoming a local legend and even a mascot for the region.

Eyewitness accounts often describe Tahoe Tessie as a large, serpent-like creature, anywhere from 10 to 80 feet in length. Its color ranges from jet black to a dark green, with a reptilian or even dinosaur-like appearance. Its undulating movement, where it creates a series of humps on the water's surface, is a hallmark of many Tessie sightings.

Noteworthy Sightings:

1. The Boater's Close Encounter (1982):

In the summer of 1982, a group of boaters reported a startling encounter. As they were enjoying the serene environment, the water beside their boat began to ripple and churn. Suddenly, a large, serpentine head emerged, its eyes seemingly staring at the group. The creature, which they estimated to be about 30 feet long, swam alongside the boat for several minutes before diving back into the depths. The shaken boaters reported the sighting to local authorities, and while no concrete evidence was found, their genuine fear and detailed description added another chapter to the Tessie legend.

2. The Deep-Sea Diver's Tale (1991):

A deep-sea diver, exploring the underwater caves of Lake Tahoe in 1991, reported a chilling encounter. As he ventured deeper into a cavern, he noticed a shadowy figure in the distance. Moving closer, he realized it was a massive creature, its body resting along the cave floor. Its eyes opened, revealing a deep blue hue, and the creature swiftly retreated further into the dark recesses of the cave. While the diver couldn't confirm it was Tessie, the sheer size and appearance of the entity left him convinced he had come face to face with the legendary creature.

Skeptics and scientists have often sought logical explanations for Tessie sightings. Some argue that the sightings could be large sturgeons or freshwater eels, both of which can grow to impressive lengths. Others suggest that the sightings might be optical illusions caused by boat wakes, floating logs, or underwater topographical features.

Lake Tahoe's depth and underwater terrain, with its many caverns and trenches, provide ample hiding places, making a comprehensive search for such a creature challenging. While no concrete evidence, such as photographic proof or biological specimens, has been presented to date, the sheer number of eyewitness accounts over the years leaves the mystery very much alive.

Tahoe Tessie has become an integral part of Lake Tahoe's cultural and economic landscape. Souvenirs bearing Tessie's image are popular among tourists, and she even has a dedicated museum exhibit. Local events and festivals often feature Tessie-themed activities, ensuring that the legend endures for each new generation.

The tales of Tahoe Tessie highlight the deep human fascination with the unknown. Whether real or folklore, Tessie serves as a reminder of nature's vast mysteries and the timeless allure of ancient legends. As long as Lake Tahoe's waters remain deep and blue, the legend of its resident serpent will continue to captivate the hearts and minds of those who visit its shores.

Ten

OTHER MYSTERIOUS CREATURES

Given its vast expanse, it's not surprising the Pacific Crest Trail has numerous legends, myths, and tales of mysterious creatures have been associated with various sections of the trail. Here are some of the creatures said to inhabit or have been seen on the PCT:

* * *

Giant Salamanders:

Giant salamanders, as their name implies, are not your average pond-dwelling creatures. While salamanders are typically small, harmless amphibians, the tales from the PCT depict a very different creature. These colossal amphibians are said to lurk in secluded ponds and slow-moving streams, particularly in the forested regions of the

Pacific Northwest. With descriptions suggesting they can grow several feet in length, they far exceed the size of any scientifically recognized salamander species in North America.

Before delving into the tales, it's essential to consider the scientific context. The world does indeed have real giant salamanders. The Chinese and Japanese giant salamanders can reach lengths of nearly six feet. These species, however, are native to parts of Asia and not the Americas.

In the regions around the PCT, the largest known salamander is the Pacific giant salamander (Dicamptodon tenebrosus), which can reach a respectable size, but typically maxes out at about a foot in length. While impressively large by salamander standards, it's not quite the behemoth depicted in legends.

-An Encounter in the Wilderness:

One genuine account that adds fuel to the giant salamander tales comes from a seasoned hiker, who in the early 2000s, recounted a startling encounter. While traversing a remote section of the PCT in Washington State, she decided to camp near a serene pond nestled among the trees. As evening settled, she heard splashes from the pond, which she initially dismissed as fish or perhaps small wildlife.

However, as she approached the water's edge, her

headlamp illuminated what she described as an "enormously thick, mottled brown creature" sliding into the pond. The length, she estimated, was close to three or four feet, and it had the unmistakable slender body and long tail of a salamander. The creature disappeared into the depths before she could snap a picture, leaving her both astonished and perplexed.

This account, shared on a hiker's forum, drew both skepticism and corroboration. Several other hikers chimed in with their own stories or mentions of local legends surrounding oversized amphibians in secluded water bodies. While no concrete evidence was provided, the sheer number of similar anecdotes was intriguing.

Is there a population of truly giant salamanders lurking in the untouched parts of the PCT? The answer remains elusive. Without photographic evidence or specimens, these creatures remain in the realm of legends. Yet, the tales persist, and for many, the possibility of such cryptic creatures adds another layer of wonder to the already majestic Pacific Crest Trail.

Thunderbirds:

The Thunderbird, a creature deeply rooted in the

legends of indigenous peoples of North America, especially those in the Pacific Northwest, is more than just a massive bird. For these cultures, the Thunderbird is a powerful spirit, an embodiment of nature's fury and majesty. With wings that create thunderclaps and eyes that flash lightning, it's no wonder that this creature is revered and feared in equal measure.

Stories describe the Thunderbird as having a wingspan several times that of a human, with powerful talons that can pick up a whale from the ocean. In many tales, Thunderbirds are seen as protectors, warding off evil spirits or great sea monsters.

As the PCT winds its way through the dense, mist-shrouded forests of the Pacific Northwest, it enters the very heartland of Thunderbird legends. Ancient totem poles carved by indigenous tribes showcase the mighty Thunderbird atop them, indicative of its dominant status in their cultural hierarchy.

Many areas along the PCT, especially in Washington State, are imbued with stories of the Thunderbird. Mount Rainier, which the PCT skirts around, is often referred to in native legends as the nesting place of these magnificent creatures.

-A Modern Encounter:

While most modern-day accounts are usually dismissive of ancient legends, considering them mere folklore, every so often a story emerges that challenges skepticism. One such tale is of a hiker in the early 2000s, trekking a remote section of the PCT near the Cascade Range in Washington.

As the hiker recounted, one evening, as a storm was brewing, he was setting up camp in a small clearing. He heard a loud, almost deafening clap of thunder, but without the preceding lightning. Looking up, he saw what he initially thought was a small plane, but soon realized it was a gigantic bird, casting a vast shadow over the land below.

The bird, he described, had a dark, almost iridescent plumage with eyes that seemed to gleam. It circled the area a few times before disappearing into the gathering clouds. While he initially hesitated to share his story, fearing ridicule, he later discovered that the region had a history of similar sightings, with locals and some older hikers nodding knowingly at his account, familiar with the tales of the Thunderbird.

While science demands evidence and cryptozoologists yearn for a conclusive proof, for many who tread the PCT, it's the experience and the stories that matter. The legend of the Thunderbird, like many other tales along this iconic trail, serves as a bridge, connecting the ancient world with the present, reminding hikers that they are mere specks in the grand tapestry of time and nature. Whether or not one believes in the Thunderbird's existence, its story undoubtedly adds another layer of mystique to the already enchanting Pacific Crest Trail.

Phantom Cats:

Phantom cats, often referred to as "alien big cats" or "black panthers" in other parts of the world, are not your typical mountain lions or bobcats that are native to the regions surrounding the PCT. These creatures are described as being larger, often with coats that are either completely black or at times, even ghostly white. The tales have persisted for decades, and while scientific evidence is scant, anecdotal accounts are numerous.

The mystery deepens when you consider that, technically, black panthers—as they are commonly depicted—are not native to North America. The term "black panther" usually refers to melanistic leopards or jaguars, species found in Africa, Asia, and South America but not in the U.S. west. So, what exactly are people seeing?

The Native American tribes that have lived in the regions surrounding the PCT have long spoken of mysterious large cats that don't fit the description of mountain lions. These creatures, sometimes considered spiritual entities or omens, are woven into the tapestry of local folklore.

-A Hiker's Tale:

One of the most intriguing accounts comes from a hiker named Jeremy, trekking the PCT in the summer of 1998. Jeremy, an experienced hiker, was no stranger to wildlife encounters. But one evening, as he was setting up camp near a water source, he noticed something unusual.

A large feline silhouette was moving stealthily near the edge of his campsite. At first, he assumed it was a curious mountain lion. However, as it came into clearer view in the dimming light, he realized its size was far greater than any mountain lion he had ever seen or heard of. Its coat was a deep shade of black, and its eyes had a peculiar, almost phosphorescent glow.

The creature lingered, watching Jeremy from a distance, its presence both majestic and eerie. After what felt like hours but was probably mere minutes, the cat slowly retreated into the dense forest. Jeremy, both awed and shaken, would recount this story at various trail stops, adding to the growing lore of the phantom cats of the PCT.

While skeptics might argue that the dim light and the solitary nature of long treks can play tricks on one's perception, tales like Jeremy's aren't isolated. Many believe that such creatures, whether they're escaped exotic pets, remnants of a species thought to be extinct, or something else entirely, roam the vast wilderness that the PCT traverses.

Attempts to validate these accounts have been numerous. Wildlife biologists, curious hikers, and local enthusiasts have tried to capture evidence of these mysterious cats. However, concrete evidence like clear photographs, tracks distinct from those of known species, or DNA samples remain elusive.

The phantom cats of the PCT are a reminder that even in an age of technology and science, some mysteries persist, lurking just beyond the periphery of understanding, waiting to be unveiled.

While the tales of these mysterious felines add an aura of intrigue to the PCT, they also serve as a cautionary note: The trail, with all its beauty, is wild and unpredictable. Whether you're an enthusiast seeking the thrill of the unknown or a hiker respecting the sanctity of nature, the stories from the PCT urge all to tread with care and reverence.

* * *

Skinwalkers:

The legend of the skinwalker originates from the Navajo culture and refers to a malevolent witch capable of transforming into, possessing, or disguising themselves as animals. The term "skinwalker" is a translation of the Navajo "yee naaldlooshii," which essentially means "by means of it, it goes on all fours." For the Navajo and some other indigenous peoples, these are not mere legends but deeply embedded aspects of their spiritual beliefs and practices, and discussing them openly is taboo.

Skinwalkers are often seen as symbols of corruption and malevolence, with the power to take over an animal's body and sometimes even human forms. Their motives are malicious, often inflicting harm, spreading disease, or causing misfortune among communities.

While the heartland of skinwalker tales lies in the desert landscapes of the Navajo Nation, stories of eerie encounters with creatures bearing similar attributes have spread to various parts. The vast, remote stretches of the PCT, especially those that wind through dense woods or pass close to indigenous lands, have become fertile ground for such tales.

-A True Tale from the Trail:

In the late 1990s, a hiker documented his solo journey along the PCT. Among his more mundane accounts of

STEVE STOCKTON & JASON KENT

wildlife encounters and the challenges of the trail, there was one entry that stood out.

It was in a stretch of dense forest in Northern California, as dusk began to fall. The hiker described the sudden drop in temperature and an inexplicable feeling of being watched. He mentioned hearing the sounds of footsteps mirroring his own but slightly out of sync, as if something was trailing him just beyond his field of vision.

As night fell, he set up camp in a small clearing. Throughout the night, he reported sounds of scratching on the outer walls of his tent and faint whispers in a language he couldn't understand. At one point, he bravely peeked out and claimed to have seen a figure— half-man, half-beast—staring intently at the tent before vanishing into the woods.

By dawn, the presence was gone. The hiker later learned about skinwalkers from a local and believed that his unsettling encounter might have been with one of these entities.

While skeptics might attribute such experiences to the heightened senses of a lone traveler in a remote location or perhaps other wild animals, for those who've felt that inexplicable dread, such explanations offer little comfort.

Stories of skinwalkers along the PCT are few and are

generally relegated to whispered campfire tales. Whether these accounts stem from genuine encounters or are merely misinterpretations of natural events embellished over time, they undeniably add another layer of depth to the mysteries of the trail.

For many indigenous communities, even speaking of skinwalkers is considered taboo, as it's believed to attract their attention. As with many such legends, whether you believe or not, respect for the cultures from which they originate and caution while venturing into unknown territories is always wise.

Chupacabra:

The legend of the Chupacabra, which translates to "goat-sucker" in Spanish, primarily originates from Latin America, particularly Puerto Rico in the mid-1990s. Described as a reptilian creature with spines or quills running down its back, the Chupacabra gets its name from its reputed habit of attacking and drinking the blood of livestock, especially goats.

While the majority of purported Chupacabra sightings hail from Latin American countries, southwestern parts of the United States, especially Texas and New Mexico, have also reported encounters. It's important to note, however,

STEVE STOCKTON & JASON KENT

that sightings along the PCT are less common, making them particularly intriguing.

Sightings of the Chupacabra along the PCT, while sparse, describe a creature somewhat different from its Latin American counterpart. Instead of the reptilian description often associated with the creature in Puerto Rico, witnesses along the PCT tend to describe a more canid creature. It often has a mangy appearance, with patches of hairless skin, and is sometimes attributed with a fierce, predatory demeanor. This appearance has led some to speculate that sightings might actually be of coyotes or other wild animals suffering from mange or other conditions.

-A Chilling Encounter: The Tale of a PCT Hiker:

In the early 2000s, a hiker named Elena documented a curious encounter while traversing a remote section of the PCT in Southern California. She had set up camp for the night, and as the sun set, she began hearing rustling noises outside her tent. At first, she dismissed it as the usual nocturnal activities of woodland creatures.

However, as the rustling grew louder and seemed to circle her tent, Elena became alarmed. She recalled the noise sounding "larger than a rabbit, but lighter-footed than a bear." Grabbing her flashlight, she unzipped her tent and shone the beam toward the disturbance.

What Elena claimed to see was a creature she couldn't readily identify. It was about the size of a large dog, but its eyes glowed an unnatural shade of red. Its skin appeared splotchy, with patches of mangy fur. Most unsettling was its posture – it seemed to be standing on its hind legs, inspecting her campsite.

The creature, seemingly startled by the flashlight, quickly bounded away, but Elena remained shaken. She later shared her story with fellow hikers and was met with mixed reactions. Some believed she might have seen a Chupacabra, while others suggested it was a sick coyote or a wild dog.

Regardless of what Elena witnessed that night, her story adds another layer to the tapestry of legends associated with the PCT.

While Chupacabra sightings are uncommon on the PCT compared to other legends, they serve as a reminder of the vast mysteries that vast stretches of wilderness like the PCT might still hold. Whether the result of misidentification, local folklore, or genuine encounters, tales like these are an integral part of the trail's mystique.

Eleven

MURDERS ON THE TRAIL

WHILE THE PACIFIC Crest Trail (PCT) is generally considered a safe place for hikers, like any location, it is not entirely without incidents of crime.

* * *

Murder on the Trail:

The trail's tranquility was shattered by a violent incident that sent shockwaves through the hiking community. Near a section of the trail in Southern California, a man launched a brutal knife attack on two hikers, leading to the tragic death of one and severely wounding the other. This chapter delves into the details of this harrowing event and its aftermath.

On the morning of May 12, 2019, two hikers were

trekking a portion of the PCT in the vicinity of Idyllwild, California. As they navigated this part of the trail, they encountered a man who appeared agitated and erratic. After a brief exchange that quickly escalated, the man attacked the pair with a knife. The male hiker, attempting to shield his female companion, bore the brunt of the assault and tragically lost his life. The female hiker sustained injuries but managed to escape and ran several miles down the trail to find help.

The assailant fled the scene but was swiftly captured by law enforcement officials. He was identified as a 30-year-old man, not previously known to the hiking community and not recognized as a regular on the PCT.

The news of the murder sent shockwaves throughout the PCT community. It was an unusual occurrence on a trail more often associated with positive and uplifting experiences. Many hikers were deeply affected, grappling with feelings of sadness, anger, and disbelief. In the immediate aftermath, some even chose to leave the trail, while others found solace in coming together, sharing stories, and supporting one another.

Law enforcement, trail organizations, and local communities organized meetings and sessions to discuss safety measures, psychological support, and methods to ensure that such an event wouldn't reoccur.

The assailant was promptly charged with murder and

attempted murder. The subsequent trial revealed more about his troubled past, though the motive for the attack remained muddled. He was eventually convicted and sentenced to life imprisonment.

While the PCT remains a haven for hikers and nature lovers worldwide, the 2019 incident served as a stark reminder that even in the most serene settings, danger could lurk. The tragedy also demonstrated the resilience and unity of the PCT community, as hikers and support groups came together to support each other, share resources, and enhance the trail's safety.

Though such violent incidents are the exception rather than the rule, they underscore the importance of taking precautions, being aware of one's surroundings, and keeping safety at the forefront when navigating the wild. The memory of the 2019 attack lingers, serving both as a somber reminder of the potential threats faced and as a testament to the strength and unity of the hiking community.

The Unsolved Mystery of the 1988 PCT Murders

Another haunting episode occurred in the summer of 1988, when two young women were found murdered near the PCT in California's San Jacinto Mountains.

On July 31, 1988, a hiker traversing a section of the PCT in the San Jacinto Mountains made a harrowing discovery. Tucked away from the main trail, near a campsite, were the lifeless bodies of two women. Both had been shot to death. The serene setting, typically a refuge for hikers and nature lovers, had become a crime scene.

The victims were identified as Patrice Reynolds, 22, and Ann Durrant, 33. Both women hailed from the San Diego area and were enjoying what was supposed to be a brief getaway to the mountains, a chance to connect with nature and escape the bustle of everyday life. They were neither thru-hikers nor were they aiming to complete the entire trail; their journey was meant to be a short escape into the wilderness.

Local law enforcement, with the assistance of the Riverside County Sheriff's Department, spearheaded the investigation. Their first task was to determine the timeline of events. When were the women last seen? Did any other hikers encounter them or notice anything unusual in the days leading up to the discovery?

Initial interviews with fellow hikers and campers painted a picture of the last known moments of Reynolds and Durrant. They were last seen alive on July 28, three days before their bodies were discovered.

One of the key challenges facing investigators was the remote location of the crime. The PCT's vastness, coupled with the rugged terrain of the San Jacinto Mountains, made gathering evidence a daunting task. Moreover, any potential witnesses would have been on the move, following the trail north or south, and possibly unaware of the investigation unfolding behind or ahead of them.

Despite the investigative challenges, authorities pursued every lead, conducting interviews and attempting to piece together the final moments of the victims. However, as days turned to months and then years, the trail grew cold.

The motives behind the killings remain a mystery. Robbery did not appear to be the motive, as some of the victims' possessions, including money, were found at the campsite. With no eyewitnesses and no strong leads pointing to a suspect, numerous questions lingered: Was it a random act of violence? Did the women encounter someone with sinister intentions while on the trail? Or was their killer someone they knew?

Decades have passed since the tragic deaths of Patrice Reynolds and Ann Durrant. Their murders remain unsolved, a somber reminder of the vulnerabilities that can exist even in places of natural beauty and serenity.

The unsolved murders of 1988, while a dark chapter in the history of the Pacific Crest Trail, serve as a reminder of the importance of safety and vigilance. While the PCT remains a beacon for hikers globally, episodes like these

STEVE STOCKTON & JASON KENT

underscore the necessity of being cautious, prepared, and ever-watchful, even in nature's embrace.

While such incidents are deeply unsettling and tragic, they are exceptions rather than the norm. The vast majority of hikers experience the PCT without any significant threat to their safety.

Twelve

MISSING PEOPLE CASES

OVER THE YEARS, several hikers and individuals have gone missing while venturing on or around the Pacific Crest Trail. While many missing persons cases are eventually resolved as lost hikers are found or their fates are discovered, others remain shrouded in mystery, contributing to the trail's lore and history. Below are some of the most well-known or intriguing cases.

* * *

The Disappearance of Kris Fowler

Known by his trail name "Sherpa", Kris embarked on the PCT with the same aspirations and dreams as countless hikers before him: to traverse its captivating expanse, to challenge himself, and to commune with nature on a profound level. But Kris's journey took a mysterious turn, leading to extensive search efforts and leaving many unanswered questions.

Kris Fowler, a native of Ohio, began his PCT hike in early 2016. By all accounts, he was an experienced hiker, someone who understood the risks and joys of long-distance trekking. As he journeyed north, he chronicled his experiences, documenting the beautiful landscapes, encounters with wildlife, and the camaraderie he found with fellow hikers.

On October 12, 2016, Kris was last seen in White Pass, Washington. It's a rugged area of the PCT, characterized by dense forests, steep terrains, and depending on the time of year, inclement weather conditions. At this point, Kris had already covered over 2,000 miles of the trail. While in White Pass, he made a brief call to his family, expressing his intent to continue onward. Unfortunately, this would be the last time his loved ones would hear from him.

Once it became clear that Kris had not checked in for an unusually extended period, concern grew. By late October, when he still hadn't made contact or reached his next expected destination, formal search efforts began. Local authorities, supported by volunteers, initiated a comprehensive search that spanned several weeks. Search dogs, helicopters, and ground teams combed the area where Kris was last believed to be.

Despite these extensive efforts, the search yielded no conclusive evidence of Kris's whereabouts. There were some reports from other hikers who believed they might have seen Kris or crossed paths with him after White Pass, but these accounts could not be definitively confirmed.

The hiking community is a tight-knit group, often coming together in times of need. In Kris's case, his disappearance resonated deeply. Fellow hikers, some of whom had met or interacted with him during his PCT journey, joined in the search. Online forums and social media groups dedicated to the PCT became hubs for information-sharing, with many sharing their own stories and encounters with Kris in hopes of piecing together his last known movements.

While the official search for Kris was eventually called off due to snow and worsening weather conditions, the mystery surrounding his disappearance remains. Some believe he might have become lost or injured in the challenging terrains after White Pass. Others speculate about potential encounters with wildlife or other unforeseen circumstances. However, without concrete evidence, it's all speculation.

Kris's family has remained hopeful, expressing their wish for answers and urging anyone with information to come forward. They've also been active in raising awareness about Kris's story, hoping that continued interest might one day lead to a breakthrough.

The tale of Kris Fowler serves as a poignant reminder of the unpredictability of nature and the risks inherent in any wilderness adventure. His story has left an indelible mark on the PCT community, forever intertwining his legacy with the trail he loved. While the questions around Kris's disappearance may remain unanswered for now, his spirit, and the hope for closure, continues to resonate with every hiker that treads the path of the Pacific Crest Trail.

The Disappearance of David O'Sullivan

David O'Sullivan hailed from Ireland, a country known for its rolling green landscapes but certainly different from the rugged terrains of the PCT. In early 2017, filled with enthusiasm and adventure, the 25-year-old decided to embark on this life-changing hike. Like many before him, David was attracted to the allure of nature, the promise of solitude, and the physical and mental challenge the PCT offers.

He began his journey in Campo, California, in March, aiming to complete the trail in five months. This would be a formidable challenge, especially for someone with limited long-hike experience like David.

David's journey, initially, was like that of many PCT hikers. He navigated through the desert sections of Southern California, enduring heat and rugged terrain. In early April, he arrived in the town of Idyllwild, a popular spot for PCT hikers to resupply and rest.

He sent an email to his family from Idyllwild, updating them on his progress and assuring them of his well-being. The O'Sullivans, like any family, were concerned for David, but this email provided them some relief. Little did they know this would be the last confirmed contact they'd have with their son.

By July, when David was scheduled to meet a friend in Santa Barbara but failed to do so, concerns for his safety began to mount. His family, who hadn't heard from him since April, started sounding the alarm bells.

The search for David was extensive. The U.S. authorities, alongside volunteers, combed areas of the PCT. Missing person posters were shared far and wide, and the PCT community became vital eyes and ears on the ground. The vast and varied terrain of the trail, ranging from scorching deserts to snow-covered mountainous regions, posed a significant challenge to the search efforts.

Given the lack of concrete leads, several theories about David's disappearance began to circulate. Some believed he might have gotten lost or injured in the challenging San Jacinto Mountains, known for its rugged terrains and potential snow during that time of the year. Others speculated about possible foul play, though no evidence supported this theory.

As weeks turned into months, the hope of finding David diminished, but the commitment to understanding his fate did not wane.

What stands out in this tragic tale is the resilience and determination of David's family. They have consistently appealed to the public for information and have maintained a presence on social media, trying to keep the memory of David's disappearance alive in people's minds.

Similarly, the PCT and the broader hiking community have exemplified solidarity. Fellow hikers, many of whom never met David, continue to share his story, always holding out hope that some information will emerge that sheds light on his whereabouts.

David O'Sullivan's disappearance is a stark reminder of the unpredictability of wilderness adventures. The PCT, with its beauty and allure, also holds areas of treacherous terrain and unpredictability.

As the years go by, the mystery of what happened to David continues. Yet, his story serves as both a cautionary tale for hikers and a testament to the strength and unity of the PCT community. His memory lives on, a beacon of hope and a reminder of the profound connections we forge with nature and each other.

* * *

The Disappearance of John Donovan

John Donovan's disappearance on the Pacific Crest Trail in 2005 is a sobering reminder of nature's unpredictability and the dangers that lurk in even the most idyllic settings. His story, though tragic, emphasizes the importance of preparation and the inherent risks of solo trekking.

In early May 2005, John Donovan, a 60-year-old experienced hiker from Virginia, embarked on a solo journey along the Pacific Crest Trail. His aim was to traverse the challenging stretch in Southern California's San Jacinto Mountains. He had tackled numerous trails in the past, but the PCT, with its diverse terrains and weather conditions, presented a unique challenge.

Before he went silent, Donovan had been regularly communicating with friends. In one of his last messages, he mentioned the impending snowstorm. This information would later prove crucial for search and rescue teams, offering a hint at what might have led to his disappearance.

When Donovan failed to check in after a few days, concerned friends alerted authorities. A massive search operation was launched, involving multiple agencies. The search teams, however, faced several challenges. The snowstorm that Donovan had mentioned had blanketed the region, obscuring tracks and altering the landscape. This made the search not only difficult but also treacherous for the rescue teams.

Despite combing through miles of the trail and its adjacent areas, the search teams found no sign of Donovan. As days turned into weeks, hopes of finding him alive began to diminish. The search was eventually called off, with Donovan presumed lost to the wilderness.

It wasn't until three years later, in 2008, that a grim discovery was made. Two hikers stumbled upon Donovan's campsite near Fuller Ridge in the San Jacinto Mountains. His tent and belongings, including a journal, were eerily preserved, almost as if frozen in time.

The journal entries provided a harrowing account of Donovan's final days. It appeared he had lost his way during the snowstorm and, realizing his dire situation, set up camp. He wrote messages to loved ones, expressing his love and his acceptance of the impending end. The notes suggested that he survived for several days before succumbing to the elements.

John Donovan's disappearance and the subsequent discovery of his campsite sent shockwaves through the hiking community. It underscored the unpredictable nature of wilderness hiking, even for seasoned hikers. Donovan's story became a cautionary tale, emphasizing the importance of preparation, understanding weather conditions, and the potential dangers of solo hikes.

While the tragedy brought grief, it also fostered a sense of community among PCT hikers. Many shared their stories, tips, and advice to ensure that fellow hikers stayed safe. Trail angels and local communities became more vigilant, offering support and assistance to those traversing the PCT.

The tale of John Donovan, like many others on the Pacific Crest Trail, is a blend of adventure, tragedy, and the indomitable human spirit. While the wilderness's allure is undeniable, his story serves as a constant reminder of the respect it demands. Today, as hikers walk the paths of the San Jacinto Mountains, many stop to remember Donovan, honoring his memory and drawing lessons from his tragic end.

* * *

The Disappearance of Stephen McGuire

In 1987, Stephen McGuire, like many before and after him, embarked on a journey to conquer the PCT. It's a decision not made lightly by anyone who takes on the challenge. Stretching over 2,650 miles from Mexico to Canada, the PCT promises both natural wonders and inevitable hardships. But Stephen was determined, and as he started his trek, he carried with him the hopes and excitement that all trail enthusiasts understand.

Details regarding Stephen's trek are unfortunately sparse. As with many hikers of the era, without the widespread use of mobile devices or GPS trackers, keeping tabs on one's location relied heavily on occasional phone calls from towns along the route or postcards sent to loved ones.

The last anyone heard from Stephen was during his journey on the PCT. His exact whereabouts, his plans, and the specific details leading up to his disappearance remain sketchy. This lack of concrete information has only added layers to the mystery.

Upon realization that Stephen had gone missing, a search was initiated. Authorities and volunteers combed sections of the trail, looking for any sign of the missing hiker. Given the PCT's vastness and the many challenges it presents—from dense forests to rugged terrains—the search proved incredibly arduous.

Days turned to weeks, then months, and eventually years. Yet, there was no trace of Stephen McGuire. No clues were discovered to indicate what might have happened or where he might have gone. The wilderness seemed to have swallowed him whole.

Over the years, hikers and those familiar with the PCT have speculated on Stephen's fate. Some believe he might have gotten lost or injured in a remote area, unable to call for help. Others theorize he could have faced unexpected severe weather conditions, an ever-present risk on the PCT. Yet others ponder the possibility of an encounter with wildlife or, less likely, foul play.

However, without tangible evidence or concrete leads, these remain mere speculations.

Stephen McGuire's disappearance stands as a haunting reminder of the unpredictability and inherent dangers of venturing into vast wilderness areas. His story is not just a mystery but also a cautionary tale, emphasizing the importance of preparation, communication, and constant vigilance on the trail.

His family and friends, while still hoping for answers, have had to grapple with the agonizing uncertainty that comes with not knowing.

* * *

The Disappearances of Rika Morita and Chaocui Wang

In 2017, the PCT community and the world at large were shaken by the separate disappearances of two young women: Rika Morita and Chaocui Wang.

-Rika Morita

Rika Morita, often known by her trail name "Strawberry," was a vibrant and enthusiastic 32-year-old hiker from Osaka, Japan. In 2017, she set out to conquer the PCT, a dream for many long-distance hikers. Rika was known to document her journey, sharing cheerful pictures and updates with her followers, showing her progress and the beautiful landscapes she traversed.

However, her journey came to an abrupt halt in California's Sierra Nevada region. The winter of 2016-2017 had been particularly heavy in terms of snowfall, making the subsequent melt-off dangerous for river crossings. In late July 2017, Rika was reported missing after she failed to meet up with friends as planned. A few days later, searchers discovered her body submerged in the South Fork of the Kings River, near Mather Pass. It's believed she may have been attempting to cross the river when the powerful currents swept her away.

-Chaocui Wang

Chaocui Wang, known on the trail as "Tree," was a 27-year-old hiker from China. Like Rika, she too was navigating the PCT in 2017, drawn to its grandeur and the challenge it presented. Chaocui, by all accounts, was a dedicated and experienced hiker, making her disappearance all the more heartbreaking.

In early August of the same year, just a few weeks after Rika Morita's tragic death, Chaocui Wang went missing in the Kings Canyon National Park, another section of the

PCT affected by the heavy snowmelt. Her last known communication was a text message sent to a friend, expressing concerns about the river crossings. A few days after the message, search teams located her body in the South Fork of the Kings River. The exact circumstances of her death remain uncertain, but given her last communication, it's believed she too fell victim to the treacherous river crossings prevalent that year.

The PCT community mourned the loss of both Rika Morita and Chaocui Wang deeply. Their tragic disappearances became a focal point for discussions about the safety of the trail, particularly concerning river crossings in high snowmelt seasons. Many hikers and PCT advocates emphasized the importance of preparation, training, and seeking local advice before attempting such crossings.

The legacies of Rika and Chaocui serve as solemn reminders of the unpredictability and inherent risks of wilderness adventures. Both women, drawn to the trail by a love of nature and a thirst for adventure, represent the spirit of the PCT. Their stories underscore the necessity of respecting nature's might, even as we marvel at its beauty.

Conclusion

As we reach the end of this journey through the legends and stories of the Pacific Crest Trail, it becomes evident that this pathway is more than just a stretch of wilderness; it is a living tapestry woven from the threads of history, culture, and the mysteries of the natural world. The tales we've explored, from the haunting allure of the Water Maidens to the ethereal Dark Watchers, stand testament to the ageless bond between humanity and the landscapes we inhabit.

These stories, while rooted in the past, speak to every traveler who treads the PCT with an open heart and a curious soul. They whisper of ancient times, of lives lived and lost, of secrets buried deep within the mountains and forests. Yet, they are not mere relics of bygone eras but living narratives that evolve, adapt, and find resonance with each new generation.

In our fast-paced, ever-changing world, the importance of such tales becomes even more pronounced. They anchor us, reminding us of the magic that exists just beyond the veil of the mundane. They teach us reverence for the land, respect for its myriad inhabitants, and the importance of preserving these natural wonders for the generations yet unborn.

For those who've walked the Pacific Crest Trail, whether in parts or its impressive entirety, the experience is transformative. The landscape, with its majestic peaks, dense forests, serene lakes, and arid deserts, etches itself into the soul. And intertwined with these physical imprints are the stories, the legends that breathe life into every rock, tree, and water body.

To the future adventurers of the PCT, may you walk with an open mind and a keen ear, for the trail speaks to those who listen. Its tales, both eerie and inspiring, await your discovery, ready to become a part of your own story.

In closing, "Legends and Stories: From the Pacific Crest Trail" is not just a recounting of myths but an invitation—a call to embrace the wonder, the mystery, and the profound connection we share with the world around us. As you close this book, may the legends live on in your heart, echoing the timeless spirit of the PCT.

- Steve Stockton

* * *

CONTINUE WITH
LEGENDS AND STORIES: FROM THE
CONTINENTAL DIVIDE TRAIL

About the Author

Steve Stockton is a veteran outdoorsman and author who has been investigating the unexplained for over 35 years. Originally from the mountains of East Tennessee, Steve has traveled all over the country and many parts of the world and now makes his home in picturesque New England with his wife, Nicole, and their dog, Mulder.

Steve cites his influences as his "gypsy witch" grand-mother, who told him multitudes of legends and stories as a small child, as well as authors such as Frank Edwards, John Keel, Charles Fort, Loren Coleman, Ivan Sanderson, Colin Wilson, and Nick Redfern.

His published books include Strange Things in the Woods (a collection of true, paranormal encounters) as well as the autobiographical My Strange World, where he talks about his own experiences dating back to childhood. Recently, he has written National Park Mysteries and Disappearances, Volumes 1, 2, and 3.

He also owns and narrates the wildly popular Among The Missing Youtube channel.

Also by Steve Stockton

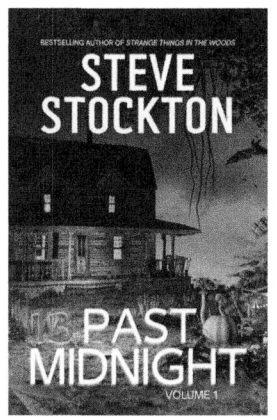

13 PAST MIDNIGHT SERIES

MYSTERIES IN THE DARK SERIES

STRANGE THINGS IN THE WOODS

MY STRANGE WORLD

NATIONAL PARK MYSTERIES & DISAPPEARANCES
SERIES

Also by Free Reign Publishing

ENCOUNTERS IN THE WOODS

WHAT LURKS BEYOND

FEAR IN THE FOREST

INTO THE DARKNESS

ENCOUNTERS BIGFOOT

TALES OF TERROR

I SAW BIGFOOT

STALKED: TERRIFYING TRUE CRIME STORIES

MYSTERIES IN THE DARK

13 PAST MIDNIGHT

THINGS IN THE WOODS

CONSPIRACY THEORIES THAT WERE TRUE

LOVE ENCOUNTERS

STAT: CRAZY MEDICAL STORIES

CRASH: STORIES FROM THE EMERGENCY ROOM

LEGENDS AND STORIES: FROM THE APPALACHIAN TRAIL

CODE BLUE: TALES FROM THE EMERGENCY ROOM

BEYOND THE PATH: TRUE TALES OF TERROR IN THE

WOODS: VOLUME 1

Printed in Great Britain
by Amazon

61316349R00099